THE FLOWERPOT FORAGER

Stuart
Ovenden

THE
FLOWERPOT
FORAGER

Hardie Grant

BOOKS

Stuart
Ovenden

Published in 2023 by Hardie Grant Books,
an imprint of Hardie Grant Publishing

Hardie Grant Books (London)
5th & 6th Floors
52–54 Southwark Street
London SE1 1UN

Hardie Grant Books (Melbourne)
Building 1, 658 Church Street
Richmond, Victoria 3121

hardiegrantbooks.com

British Library Cataloguing-in-Publication
Data. A catalogue record for this book
is available from the British Library.

The Flowerpot Forager
ISBN: 978-1-78488-625-7

10 9 8 7 6 5 4 3 2 1

Publishing Director: Kajal Mistry
Acting Publishing Director: Emma Hopkin
Commissioning Editor: Eve Marleau
Senior Editor: Eila Purvis
Design, Art Direction and illustration:
A+B Studio (Amelia Leuzzi + Bonnie Eichelberger)
Copy-editor: Lucy York
Proofreader: Suzanne Juby
Fact checker: Sarah Watson
Production Controller: Gary Hayes

Colour reproduction by p2d
Printed and bound in China by
Leo Paper Products Ltd.

Introduction

This book was not conceived as, nor is it intended to be, a replacement for the much-loved pastime of gathering wild food in the great outdoors. Foraging, a pursuit once practised by our ancestors out of necessity, is today a common hobby for culinary enthusiasts with an interest in free, locally sourced food. The presence of wild ingredients in food culture continues to gather momentum. To call foraging a hobby is not to undermine its historical importance or belittle its many virtues; it reflects the ease at which humans can obtain food in the 21st century. I am unlikely ever to need to hunt for wild leaves, berries or roots as an exclusive means of providing sustenance for my family, but I have always considered a foray into the wild in search of food to be an immersive and contemplative experience – good for the mind, body and soul.

So why, then, grow wild food at home? There have been times in recent years when venturing out into the wider world has seemed like a luxury to us all. I started my collection over three years ago at the beginning of the pandemic, with a little pot of wood sorrel. I reasoned that if I couldn't forage for it in the wild at the time, I'd forage for it in the garden. Horseradish and water mint were planted soon after, as were the first dandelion and perennial wall rocket seeds. It wasn't long until I could harvest my first wild ingredients. Every new seedling or shoot brought with it the sense that this wasn't purely a project to undertake during a period of confinement, but a positive way to garden at any time, in any place. There are a number of reasons why you should consider growing your own edible wild plants.

Location

While many people live within a short walk or drive from a field, meadow or hedgerow, this isn't always the case, especially for those who live in towns and cities. The same goes for the coast; my own forays to the beach are few and far between – I live over an hour's drive from the nearest salt marsh and the reality is that I'll probably pick wild marsh samphire once or twice a year (if I'm lucky). With this book I hope to explore the idea that eating fresh wild food isn't necessarily dictated by geographic position.

Safety

It takes time and patience to accumulate the knowledge required to forage safely and, even then, the margins for error can be small. Many people have concerns about gathering wild food, fearing that they might get it wrong. Mother Nature can be very indifferent to casual mistakes – you should never eat anything picked from the wild if you aren't completely sure what it is. It took me many years to be able to positively identify the subtle differences between cow parsley (tasty), sweet cicely (even tastier) and hemlock (deadly), and even now with certain plants and fungi it's easy to have a taxonomological wobble. Peace of mind is a good thing; every wild plant that I have grown in the garden during the past 2 years has been either raised from seed or grown from a 100 per cent positively identified rhizome or cutting.

The law

It is illegal to intentionally uproot any wild plant in the UK without the landowner's permission, which can put certain forageables, such as burdock, horseradish, ramsons and reedmace into a sketchy realm in terms of legitimate acquisition. The four Fs – flowers, foliage, fruit and fungi – may be picked for personal use, but some plants, such as Bristol onion, are protected by law. There are plenty of grey areas out there when it comes to foraging, which are easily avoided in the comfort of your own garden.

Environmental considerations

I have recently started to ask myself the question – just because I can pick a basket of leaves or flowers on a forage, does it mean that I should? Our meadows, woodlands, rivers and hedgerows are being placed under extraordinary levels of strain; it's reasonable to say that many aren't doing particularly well. Climate change, habitat loss, pesticide use, pollution – all have had a direct impact on the flora and fauna that share the world with us. The past 20 years have seen shocking declines in insect numbers, which are fundamental to a healthy environment, while many mammal, bird, reptile and amphibian populations are also in trouble. Foraging with care and restraint has never been more important. Perhaps we should be adding to the ecosystem, rather than taking from it? Since I have been growing wild plants in the garden, the increase in wildlife has been notable, from honeybees bustling around borage flowers in search of nectar, to wood pigeons hanging around the chickweed trug, hoping for a quick snack. Many of the plants in this book are native, after all, so it makes perfect sense that they are attractive to local wildlife. I can usually spare a little of my crop and still have more than enough left to eat.

Getting started

Growing a wild plant successfully in a pot is essentially an exercise in recreating its native environment on a small scale, whether it be a shady wooded nook, patch of wasteland or wet river margin. Shade-loving plants generally favour soil that retains a bit of moisture, while those in full sun prefer free-draining soil and are slightly more tolerant to drought. If your outdoor area is south facing, it is unlikely that plants such as ramsons, sweet cicely or wood sorrel will thrive, while sun lovers such as wild fennel and borage are unlikely to produce healthy crops if positioned in a dark corner. Be led by your space; there are plants in this book that will grow in all aspects.

Soil and kit

I make a point of only ever using peat-free compost, mixing in either perlite, sand or grit to improve drainage where necessary. Variations on compost type (ericaceous, for example) are listed where appropriate. There is no need to get bogged down in posh kit; aside from a few pots, a good sturdy trowel and a watering can, you really don't need much else to get started.

Choosing a pot or container

For the most part, it's a case of the bigger the better, and it doesn't necessarily matter what you use as a growing vessel, providing it has drainage holes. Buckets, wine crates, colanders – there was a point last summer when I had over a dozen wild strawberry plants growing in an old cattle trough; they loved it, spilling enthusiastically over the edges and returning a good crop all summer long. The more individual plants that you can get in a pot or container, providing they are adequately spaced apart, the higher the yield will be. Trees

and some of the larger herbaceous perennials are exceptions
as they often need to be planted singly, while some of the
more petite plants will be more than happy in a relatively small
pot. One thing I do tend to avoid is plastic. There are plenty
of options out there that are far better for the environment;
terracotta pots can be used again and again, as can materials
such as aluminium and wood, which can also be recycled.

A note on eating wild plants

The general rule for testing an edible plant, new to you (which
has been safely identified), is to try a little, then wait 24 hours
before eating it again. This isn't about a risk of being poisoned;
many people are unaware of food allergies or intolerances
until they first present themselves, so a little hesitance at
the beginning is always advised. Pregnant or breastfeeding
women and people taking prescribed medicine should seek
advice from a professional before consuming wild plants.

Recipes

The recipes listed in this book are very much the tip of
the iceberg in terms of unlocking the culinary potential
of these wild ingredients. I have found that the trick
is to make them prominent in the dish and try not to
bury them among lots of strong additional flavours.
Experimentation is key; all of the plants listed have been
consciously chosen for their versatility in the kitchen.

Finally

When you grow a plant to maturity from a seed, root or
cutting, you can't help but learn from it. This might take
the form of a simple observation – noticing a change
in colour of a seed head, the way in which growth dies
back in winter, or the curl of a new shoot in spring.
I have reached a point with my potted wild larder where I am
reasonably self-sufficient in terms of small-scale gathering.
Moving forwards, I plan to balance this garden-based resource
with conventional forays in search of food – the margin of
distinction between wild and home cultivated needn't be
a big one. Growing wild plants at home helps to further
an understanding of them, which in turn will make us all
better foragers when we venture back out into the wild.

Horseradish

Horseradish is an attractive plant that is perfectly at home as part of potted planting scheme, even before one starts to consider unlocking its culinary potential. The leaves are fast growing, architectural and vibrant, bringing a welcome splash of fresh green to any patio or terrace.

GROW

It is best to grow horseradish as an annual. Small sections of horseradish root, or thongs, are readily available online and from specialist nurseries in early spring. A deep pot is essential; horseradish roots can grow to over a metre (3 ft) long, but a 25-litre (6.6-gallon) pot will return a nicely sized root and house up to three plants. A 4:1 mix of compost and horticultural sand gives the plant a loose, well-drained environment in which to grow – take care to remove any stones or lumps which might cause the root to fork. Plant the thongs approximately 5 cm (2 in) deep and water in well.

CARE

Water horseradish regularly and treat it to a feed with a balanced liquid fertiliser in early summer. Horseradish does well in both full sun and partial shade but ensure that it doesn't dry out. Trim off any shabby or withered leaves to keep the plant looking neat and tidy.

EAT

Young leaves can be finely shredded and used to finish stir-fries and sushi dishes. Steaming or blanching slightly older leaves (tough stems removed) removes hotness, after which they can be used in shakshukas, tortillas and risottos. Flowers can be used as a garnish. The grated root is most commonly used in the preparation of horseradish sauce, which is a classic accompaniment to roast beef.

WILDLIFE

Despite its fiery kick, it is not uncommon to find caterpillars on the leaves in late summer and they can quickly strip a plant if left to their own devices. Horseradish is a member of the *Brassicaceae* family, which, as every keen cabbage grower will know, can be problematic in terms of garden wildlife. Carefully move them onto a similar food plant that you don't mind getting eaten – I often underplant horseradish with nasturtiums to provide an alternative for native species.

CAUTIONS

While both the leaves and the root are perfectly edible, they should only be consumed in small quantities. One tends to use horseradish sparingly, so overdoing it is unlikely. Wear gloves when grating roots as the volatile oils can irritate skin. Avoid periods of regular consumption if pregnant, breastfeeding or suffering from low thyroid function.

Horseradish pickled cucumbers

This is a slightly more unusual way of using horseradish, but the spicy kick really does come through in the cucumbers. I often add a splash of the pickling brine to a Bloody Mary cocktail, which is a trusted friend of horseradish.

MAKES 1 LARGE JAR —

300 g (10½ oz) small cucumbers, halved or quartered (depending on size)

2 teaspoons flaky sea salt

250 ml (8½ fl oz) white wine vinegar

250 ml (8½ fl oz) water

50 g (2 oz) caster (superfine) sugar

decent-sized chunk of horseradish root, peeled and grated

1 teaspoon wild fennel seeds (optional)

STEP 1 —

Spread the cucumbers out in a tray, then scatter over the sea salt. Cover loosely with a sheet of baking parchment, then sit in a cool place overnight.

STEP 2 —

Drain off any liquid from the tray, give the cucumbers a quick rinse with cold water then transfer to a large, sterilised jar. Bring the vinegar, water and sugar to a simmer, then remove from the heat. Stir in the horseradish and fennel seeds (if using), then pour the liquid over the cucumbers, ensuring that they are completely covered. Store in a cool, dark place until ready to use.

Common elder

The sight of the first elderflower in mid to late May seems to mark a point of transition, from the lush green growth of spring with its spill of tender leaves and delicate flowers, to the sun-scorched haze of summer. My potted elder sits in the front garden where it gets sunlight all day; given adequate water it is perfectly happy and provides me with enough flowers each year for a number of recipes. Leave half of the flowers on the tree; you don't need as many as you think and you will be rewarded with a small crop of berries in autumn (fall).

GROW

There is little entertainment value to be derived from extracting the tiny seed from an elderberry – your best bet is to take softwood cuttings in early summer, before flowering. Identify a healthy-looking parent plant and use sharp secateurs to remove 15–20-cm (6–8-in) stem lengths, cutting horizontally below a bud for the base of the cutting and at a 45-degree angle above a bud for the top. Choose smooth, healthy-looking branches from the current year's growth and remove all but a couple of leaves at the top. Dip the bottom of each cutting in hormone rooting powder and insert into small pots filled with perlite, leaving two-thirds of the cutting exposed. Sit on a warm, bright windowsill out of direct sunlight. Keep the perlite moist and give the cuttings a mist with water every few days. Cuttings will be ready to be transferred to small pots after roughly 8 to 10 weeks. You will know they are ready when they offer a resistance when tugged gently, indicating that they have taken root.

Elder has a relatively shallow root system and doesn't need a huge pot to grow well, although a reasonable amount of width is required to allow the roots to grow laterally. A 40 x 30 cm (12 x 15¾ in) pot is perfect for a small patio or balcony. Establish young elder plants in a 4:1 mix of mature plant compost and horticultural grit for good drainage. Mulch the top of the pot and keep an eye out for weeds, which can easily choke the shallow root system.

Position in either full sun or partial shade; flower and fruit yields will be lower if the plant doesn't get enough sunlight.

CARE

Elder likes moist soil, so ensure that it doesn't dry out. Due to its shallow-rooting nature, one can safely assume that if the top of the soil is dry when touched, the roots are also dry. Regular watering in the summer months is essential, as trees will not withstand a period of drought. Feed in spring with an all-purpose continuous-release plant food.

Elders grown from cuttings should flower and fruit for the first time 2 years after planting. A light winter prune can help to retain shape, but avoid cutting back hard, as this will stimulate stem and leaf growth at the expense of flower and berry production. Remove any suckers that spring up from the root system.

EAT

Elderflowers are used to make the queen of summer syrups – elderflower cordial. This can be used in drinks, ice creams, vinegars and jellies. The flavour is unique; gooseberries are a particularly good seasonal pairing. The flowers can also be made into fritters.

Elderberries can be made into cordials, vinegars and jellies, all of which can be used in both savoury and sweet dishes. The berries are high in vitamin C and antioxidants – many believe that a spoonful of elderberry cordial a day keeps winter colds and flu away.

WILDLIFE

This year my potted elder has become home to a tiny green orb-weaver spider (*Araniella cucurbitina*), which despite its almost fluorescent green abdomen, is perfectly camouflaged inside the busy network of slender oval leaflets. Elder also plays host to several moth caterpillars, while the flowers provide nectar for a variety of insects. Small mammals such as dormice may take advantage of the berries, as will birds, so try to get there before them if planning to harvest.

CAUTIONS

Elderberries need to be cooked and should not be eaten raw. The plant's stems are rather toxic if ingested without cooking. This is not the case with the flowers. Seek guidance from your doctor if eating regularly alongside prescribed medication, or are pregnant or breastfeeding. The leaves and twigs are not edible as they contain toxic levels of cyanogenic glucosides.

A small bottle of elderflower cordial

You don't need many flower heads to enjoy homemade elderflower cordial. Most recipes start with a hefty 1.5 litres (50 fl oz) of water, and while I love nothing more than a cool elderflower spritzer on a hot day, that is a lot of cordial to drink. Far better to view it as a fleeting seasonal treat at the height of the season – a bit like asparagus – then look forward to elderberries in autumn (fall).

STEP 1 —

Give the elderflowers a quick look over to remove any hidden bugs. Bring the sugar and water to a near-simmer in a saucepan (keep the lid on to reduce water evaporation), then remove from the heat. Pare the zest from the lemon with a potato peeler, then cut the fruit into slices. Pour the hot sugar water into a bowl, then stir in the elderflowers, lemon zest, slices and citric acid. Cover the bowl with a clean tea towel (dish towel) and leave to infuse for 24 hours.

STEP 2 —

Strain the cordial through a piece of clean muslin (cheesecloth), then use a funnel to pour the liquid into a sterilised bottle. The cordial will keep in the refrigerator for about 6 weeks.

MAKES 1 SMALL BOTTLE—

5 large elderflower heads

600 g (1 lb 5 oz) granulated sugar

400 ml (13 fl oz) water

1 lemon

¼ teaspoon citric acid

Steamed asparagus with elderflower, cucumber and gooseberry dressing

I love this recipe because it's unusual; I also love the fact that it's one of those dishes that is very much of the moment – you'd struggle to make it any time of the year other than early summer.

SERVES 4 AS A SIDE DISH —

¼ cucumber, deseeded and diced

50 g (2 oz) gooseberries, thinly sliced

2 tablespoons elderflower cordial

2 tablespoons olive oil

juice of ½ lemon

a couple sprigs of sweet cicely, chopped (optional)

200 g (7 oz) asparagus spears

sea salt and freshly ground black pepper

TO SERVE —

a few elderflowers

STEP 1 —

Mix the cucumber, gooseberries, cordial, oil, lemon juice and cicely together in a bowl, then season to taste. Set aside for at least 10–15 minutes before serving, to let the flavours mingle.

STEP 2 —

Steam the asparagus for 3–6 minutes, or until a sharp knife slips easily through a spear. Transfer to a serving dish, then spoon over the dressing. Finish with a few elderflowers, pinched off the tree.

Borage

It's only when you start exploring the heritage of the edible plants that are to be found in the wild that you learn that many of them aren't native. Some have become naturalised after being brought over by occupiers such as the Romans and Normans, while others escaped from gardens. One such plant is pineapple weed (*Matricaria discoidea*), a widespread member of the chamomile family that many believe left Kew Gardens rather surreptitiously in the tread of a car tyre. Another is borage. Borage is native to the Mediterranean and loves a bit of heat; I grow it against a south-facing wall, keep it well watered and it provides me with flowers all summer long.

GROW

Sow borage seeds in spring, after the last frosts have passed. Sow seeds 2 cm (¾ in) deep, 5 cm (2 in) apart in trays filled with a 4:1 mix of compost and perlite. Prick out seedlings once the first two true leaves have formed, then transfer to small pots. Pot on once a strong root system is established – a large pot filled with a 4:1 mix of compost and horticultural grit should keep up to five borage plants more than happy. Borage thrives in full sun, although it will tolerate partial shade.

CARE

Borage does best in soil with low fertility; there is no need to add organic matter or feed the plants. Water regularly during hot periods. Remove faded flower heads to encourage new bud growth and to prevent the plant self-seeding. Borage is an annual; stems and leaves can be composted but always dispose of spent flowers and seed heads separately.

EAT

Flowers finish a salad, savoury tart or cake with a wonderful pop of colour and a gentle cucumber flavour – they can also be frozen into ice cubes for use in chilled drinks. Leaves and stems are suitable for occasional use and are great in soups and stir-fries.

WILDLIFE

Borage will be visited again and again by pollinating insects during the summer months. One scorching afternoon in July last year, I discovered a hummingbird hawk-moth (*Macroglossum stellatarum*) darting about the flowers in a blur of orange and grey, probing for nectar with its long proboscis. It was a joy to watch, an event that brought everyone outside from the house for a moment to marvel at its hurried quest for sustenance.

CAUTIONS

Borage could be confused with Russian comfrey (*Symphytum x uplandicum*) which can have blue flowers and has PAs in higher quantities than borage, so it's not safe to consume. Make sure the flowers are star-shaped, rather than tubular.

While they are also edible, borage stems and leaves contain pyrrolizidine alkaloids. They are present in such small quantities that small levels of consumption are thought to be harmless, but pregnant or breastfeeding women and those with liver problems are advised not to eat borage, as a precaution.

Borage borek

I make this stuffed filo pastry wheel regularly and often mix up the filling, depending on what is in season at the time. Nettles, ramsons (ramps) and sea beet also work well in place of borage.

STEP 1 —

The night before, place a sieve lined with muslin (cheesecloth) over a small bowl. Spoon in the ricotta, gather the cloth over the cheese and place a weight on top. Leave in the refrigerator overnight; in the morning there should be a pool of liquid in the bowl and the cheese should be much thicker, with a crumbly texture.

STEP 2 —

Heat 1 tablespoon of the oil in a pan, then fry the shallots for 15–20 minutes on a low heat until softened, golden and sticky. Spoon the shallots into a bowl. Rinse the borage and spinach in cold water, then drain. Cook in the remaining tablespoon of oil for 7–10 minutes until wilted. Leave to cool.

STEP 3 —

Squeeze out as much water as you can from the cooked leaves. Give them a rough chop, then stir into the shallots, ricotta, garlic, lemon juice and a good pinch of salt and pepper. Set to one side.

STEP 4 —

Preheat the fan oven to 180°C (350°F/gas 6). Lay a sheet of filo flat on a clean surface, then brush one of the short ends with the melted butter. Attach a second sheet and overlap the two sheets by roughly 10 cm (4 in). Brush both sheets with the butter, then place two more sheets on top.

STEP 5 —

Spoon the borage and spinach mixture along one of the long sides of the pastry, roughly 3 cm (1⅛ in) from the edge. Roll the pastry up into a long sausage, then shape into a spiral – approximately 17 cm (6½ in) in size. Carefully transfer the borek to a buttered cake tin (pan) or round, ovenproof dish. Brush generously with the egg, sprinkle over the sesame seeds then bake in the oven for 40–45 minutes until golden. Serve warm, with a salad of wild leaves.

SERVES 2 —

150 g (5 oz) ricotta

2 tablespoons rapeseed (canola) oil

3 banana shallots, chopped

250 g (9 oz) borage leaves

250 g (9 oz) spinach leaves

2 teaspoon garlic granules

juice of ½ lemon

salt and freshly ground black pepper

4 sheets filo pastry

125 g (4 oz) unsalted butter, melted

1 egg, beaten

1 teaspoon sesame seeds

Meadowsweet

Meadowsweet is a handsome plant with long, elegant leaf stems and a froth of off-white flowers that almost look like daubs of clotted cream along the riverbank when they begin to appear in midsummer. The flowers are deeply fragrant; historically they were strewn across floors to perfume rooms and it is documented that they were greatly favoured by Elizabeth I in her bedchamber. My potted *Filipendula ulmaria* is three years old and comes back just as strong every spring.

GROW

Sow meadowsweet in autumn (fall), using seed trays filled with a 4:1 mix of compost and perlite. Cover seeds with a thin layer of soil, then sit the pot in a sheltered spot out of the worst of the weather. Keep the soil moist during the winter months.

Prick out seedlings after the first true leaves have formed, then grow on in smaller pots. Transfer established plants into large pots, filled with a 4:1 mix of compost and horticultural grit.

CARE

Meadowsweet is a plant of riverbanks, damp meadows and ditches, and while good drainage is preferable in the pot or container, it loves wet environments. Keep well-watered – if anything, overwater it. A feed with a liquid fertiliser in early spring will encourage strong growth.

Cut back the leaves in late autumn (fall); mulch with a layer of leaf mould and sit in a sheltered spot during the winter months. Bring it out again in the spring; meadowsweet is hardy and should come back year after year.

EAT

Flowers infuse well into custards, ice creams and panna cottas – the flavour is floral and complex, with a touch of almond. Make sure to harvest flowers on a hot, sunny day to catch them at their best.

Leaves have a bright, wintergreen note and are a great addition to salads. They can also be sautéed, added to soups and used to flavour stewed fruit and summer punches. The leaves dry well but take care to do this quickly before storing in an airtight container.

WILDLIFE

Meadowsweet attracts a whole host of insects, including bees, butterflies and moths. It is one of the food plants of the emperor moth (*Saturnia pavonia*), which is one of the UK's largest insects and has striking, eye-like spots on its wings – a bit like the peacock butterfly (*Aglais io*).

CAUTIONS

Meadowsweet contains salicylates, which may act as an anticoagulant if taken in high enough doses. The plant is generally considered safe and is widely used in small amounts.

Meadowsweet custard tart

Meadowsweet infuses well into custard, milk or cream and this tart is a great way of introducing friends or family to its distinct flavour.

STEP 1 —

Whizz the butter, flour, salt, sugar and lemon zest together in a food processor until you have a breadcrumb-like consistency, then transfer to a bowl. Stir in the egg yolk and 1 tablespoon of cold water, then bring together into a dough. Wrap the pastry in cling film (plastic wrap) and chill in the refrigerator for a minimum of 1 hour.

STEP 2 —

Roll the pastry out on a lightly floured surface to a 5-mm (¼-in) thickness, then use it to line a 20-cm (8-in) tart tin, leaving 2–3-cm (¾–1⅛-in) of pastry overhang at the edge. Chill in the refrigerator for another hour.

STEP 3 —

Preheat the fan oven to 170°C (325°F/gas 5). Line the pastry case with baking parchment and baking beans, then bake blind for 20 minutes. Remove the beans and parchment, then bake for a further 15 minutes or until the base is golden and biscuity.

STEP 4 —

Make the filling. Bring the cream, vanilla extract and meadowsweet flowers to the boil, remove from the heat, then remove the flowers with a slotted spoon. Add the sugar and egg yolks to a large, heatproof bowl. Mix with a wooden spoon until pale. Slowly drizzle in the hot cream, a little at a time, stirring continuously (don't whisk). Strain the custard through a fine sieve into a jug.

STEP 5 —

Reduce the oven to 130°C (270°F/gas 2). Trim off the excess pastry, then sit the tin on a baking tray (pan). Pull the middle shelf of the oven out halfway, sit the tray on the shelf, then pour in the custard. Carefully slide the shelf back in and bake the tart for 45–60 minutes, or until the custard is just set with a slight wobble. Leave to cool completely in the tin, then serve with a scattering of strawberries and a dusting of icing sugar.

SERVES 8 —

FOR THE PASTRY —

75 g (2½ oz) unsalted butter

150 g (5 oz) plain (all-purpose) flour

pinch of sea salt

50 g (2 oz) icing (confectioner's) sugar, plus extra for dusting

zest of 1 lemon

1 egg yolk

FOR THE FILLING —

600 g (1 lb 5 oz) double (heavy) cream

¼ teaspoon vanilla extract

4–5 meadowsweet flower heads

100 g (3½ oz) caster (superfine) sugar

8 egg yolks

TO SERVE —

handful of strawberries (use wild, if growing), chopped

Water mint

Water mint is a fast-growing, herbaceous perennial that is very easy to grow. I tend to start plants in a pond basket, but even a few stems poked into a glass of water on a bright windowsill will have sprouted roots in next to no time, after which they can be potted up. Many people will have mint growing in the garden, but it's always nice to try something different and *Mentha aquatica* has its own unique mint flavour.

GROW

Left to its own devices, water mint spreads vigorously via fleshy, underground rhizomes. It needs to be kept in check, which makes it the perfect plant to grow in a container (as I find is the case with all mints). Take cuttings in spring from established plants, approximately 10 cm (4 in) in length. Cut just below a leaf node and remove all but the top few leaves.

Fill a pond basket with aquatic pond compost, keeping the level to about 2.5 cm (1 in) below the rim. Insert the cuttings into the soil, leaving about 4 cm (1½ in) of stem above the compost and spacing approximately 10 cm (4 in) apart. Gently cover the surface of the soil with washed agricultural grit; this is to prevent the soil dissipating when it is submerged in water.

Lower the basket onto a shallow ledge in a pond, or into a large container filled with rainwater. Position in full sun or partial shade; cuttings will have taken root after a couple of weeks and new growth will be noticeable soon after.

CARE

Water mint requires little in the way of regular care. It can start to look a bit tired and leggy towards the end of summer; a light prune with secateurs can help neaten it up and stimulate new growth. Deadhead flowers to prevent it self-seeding and cut back hard in late autumn (fall) – it'll grow back again the following spring.

EAT

A little water mint goes a long way; it has a stronger flavour than many cultivated mints and while, it does have distinct minty notes, there is also a touch of aniseed in there. Use it in cocktails, ice creams and teas, stir it into savoury rice and pasta dishes or chop into ribbons and add to summer fruit salads. Flowers can be used as a garnish.

WILDLIFE

Water mint flowers are incredibly attractive to butterflies, especially the comma (*Polygonia c-album*). The comma is a fascinating butterfly, with ragged-looking wing edges and tiny white markings on the ventral wing sides that, rather unsurprisingly, look like comma punctuation marks.

CAUTIONS

There are no direct concerns when using members of the mint family (*Lamiaceae*) as a culinary ingredient, but when harvesting *Mentha aquatica* from a pond to eat ensure that leaves are only picked from above the water line and wash well before using.

Water-mint mojito

You can't beat a good mojito. Take care not
to add too much soda water at the end; it's
easy to get carried away, fill it to the brim
and inadvertently over-dilute the drink.

MAKES 1 DRINK —

½ lime, cut into
4 long wedges

juice of ½ lime

6–8 water mint
leaves, plus an extra
sprig to serve

1 teaspoon caster
(superfine) sugar

handful of
crushed ice

50 ml (1¾ fl oz)
white rum

soda water

STEP 1 —

Add the lime wedges, juice, mint leaves and
sugar to a sturdy highball glass, then give the fruit
a gentle squash, or 'muddle' with the end of a clean
rolling pin or the back of a wooden spoon.

STEP 2 —

Add the ice, then pour over the rum.
Top the glass up with a little soda water,
then finish with a sprig of water mint.

Lesser burdock

I grow *Arctium minus* as much for the ornamental beauty of the leaves as I do the edible root. They are large, architectural and have an almost prehistoric look about them; any potted planting scheme with a semi-tropical feel will benefit from the inclusion of a few burdock plants.

GROW

Burdock is a biennial and is best harvested in either its first autumn (fall) or second spring. In late winter, sow seeds indoors in trays filled with a 4:1 mix of compost and perlite, 6 cm (2⅜ in) apart, 3 cm (1⅛ in) deep. Sit the tray somewhere bright and water regularly. Carefully transfer seedlings into small individual pots once the first two true leaves have formed, then grow on until plants are well established. Harden off in a cold frame, then space 20 cm (8 in) apart in large containers or troughs (the deeper, the better) filled with a 4:1 mix of multipurpose compost and horticultural sand. Once planted, position burdock in full sun or partial shade.

CARE

Keep well-watered during hot spells – burdock is a thirsty plant that needs hydration for the roots to grow to a good size. Regular slug patrols may be necessary as the creatures do have a predilection for the tender young leaves. A midsummer feed with a multipurpose fertiliser is beneficial but not essential. Cut back any dead growth in December/January if overwintering.

If by any chance the plant is left to flower and produce seed heads in its second year, carefully remove the spiky burrs and discard – do not compost.

EAT

Young burdock leaves are very bitter but they can be used as a spinach substitute. The stems are also edible, although it's best to eat the young flowering stems, because they can become woody and bitter. The best part of burdock is the root. It's important to scrub the roots well to remove any dirt, after which they can be used in a similar way to parsnips – boiled for use in mashes and purées or roasted in the oven.

Burdock root is prevalent in Chinese and Japanese cuisine, so it's of little surprise that it lends itself well to stir-fries, spicy braised dishes and aromatic broths. Prep the roots *sasagaki*-style, or by julienning. Sasagaki is a Japanese way of chopping, whereby thin splinters are sliced off the root while it is held at the base, in a similar way to how you sharpen a pencil with a knife.

Burdock root can be used in cordials and home brews, either on its own, or paired in time-honoured tradition with dandelion.

WILDLIFE

Burdock flowers are known to attract bees and insects, but if growing as a food crop the plant is unlikely to reach this point. Slugs are of course an important part of the garden ecosystem and are likely to be attracted to the leaves; whether they are welcome in this instance is debatable, but birds such as the blackbird (*Turdus merula*) and magpie (*Pica pica*) will eat them and they are always welcome in the garden.

CAUTIONS

Burdock has been known to cause allergic reactions in people who are sensitive to the *Asteraceae/Compositae* family, which includes lettuce, calendula and tarragon.

Quick-braised burdock and carrots

This dish is popular in Japan, where it is known as *kinpira gobō*. I like to serve it with steamed fish, but it also works well with chicken or pork.

SERVES 2 AS A SIDE —

200 ml (7 fl oz) dashi stock

2 tablespoons soy sauce

2 tablespoons mirin

1 tablespoon sesame oil

1 large burdock root, cut sasagaki-style

2 carrots, julienned

½ red chilli, deseeded and finely chopped

½ teaspoon caster (superfine) sugar

TO SERVE —

pinch of shichimi tōgarashi

½ teaspoon white sesame seeds

½ teaspoon black sesame seeds

STEP 1 —

Mix the stock, soy sauce and mirin in a bowl and set to one side.

STEP 2 —

Heat the sesame oil in a wok or large frying pan, then stir-fry the burdock, carrot, chilli and sugar for 2–3 minutes on a medium heat. Pour in the flavoured stock, then cook for a further 2 minutes, or until the liquid has almost gone.

STEP 3 —

Serve with shichimi tōgarashi and sesame seeds sprinkled on top.

Wild strawberry

I have a fond memory of walking down a quiet country lane in Dorset about 10 years ago, with my daughter picking wild strawberries as the evening sun dipped over the Axe Vale; they tasted so good. I've grown *Fragaria vesca* at home ever since – once you've tried one, you'll struggle to go back to its plumper, cultivated cousins.

GROW

Sow wild strawberry seeds indoors in February. Lightly sow seeds onto a pre-watered tray filled with a 4:1 mix of compost and perlite, then lightly cover with soil. Sit the tray on a warm bright windowsill out of direct sunlight and keep the soil moist with a spray bottle. Transfer seedlings into individual pots once the first two true leaves have formed, then grow on until plants are well established and a good root network has formed. Harden off in a cold frame before potting on – preferably after the last frosts have passed.

Strawberries prefer slightly acidic soil, so plant in a 3:1 mix of multipurpose and ericaceous compost. Trugs and window boxes are perfect for growing wild strawberries on a balcony or patio, but any pot or container will do. Space the plants 5 cm (2 in) apart and water in well. Position in full sun or partial shade, but bear in mind that fruit yields will be greater the more sun they get.

New plants can also be propagated in late spring and summer from stolons – thin runners that feel their way out from the main plant and root where they touch the ground. Simply lift the runner up and look for tiny roots at the base of the leaf node. Gently rest the node on a new pot filled with compost, wait for it to take root, then cut away the stem from the main plant.

CARE

Give the plants a feed with liquid tomato food in spring once they have begun to flower, then again in autumn (fall) after the last strawberry of the year has been picked. Water regularly during hot periods. Cut back any dead and withered growth in late autumn (fall), mulch with a layer of leaf mould, then tuck away somewhere sheltered. *Fragaria vesca* is a perennial and should come back year after year.

EAT

Wild strawberries are much smaller than regular strawberries, but what they lack in size they more than make up for in flavour. Each berry pops with such an intense burst of sweetness that they can make some of their cultivated cousins seem bland in comparison. The reason that wild strawberries aren't to be found in shops and supermarkets is that they don't keep; a few hours after picking they are already past their best.

While the harvest from a window box or container might not be adequate to make a batch of jam, half a dozen or so plants will provide more than enough berries for a number of summer dishes. Scatter over pavlovas, jellies and ice creams, or macerate in a little sugar and lemon juice before spooning over a bowl of breakfast yoghurt in the morning.

WILDLIFE

If you're lucky (and I do mean lucky), you may find small green caterpillars nibbling on your wild strawberry leaves in midsummer. *Fragaria vesca* is one of the favoured food plants of the grizzled skipper (*Pyrgus malvae*), a handsome little butterfly that, like many native insect species, is in decline due to loss of habitat.

CAUTIONS

Take caution if allergic to other fruits in the *Rosaceae* family, such as raspberries, cherries and apples.

Wild strawberry vinegar

This vinegar is great in salad dressings or even drinks. Add a splash to the bottom of a glass, throw in a few ice cubes then top up with chilled sparkling water.

STEP 1 —

Toss the strawberries in a small bowl with the sugar, pop a plate on the bowl and leave at room temperature for 24 hours – the fruit should start to break down and ferment, which boosts flavour.

STEP 2 —

Pour over the vinegar, then give the fruit a gentle mash with a fork. Leave to infuse for a further 24 hours, then strain the liquid through a fine sieve. Pour the strawberry vinegar into a sterilised jar and refrigerate until ready to use.

MAKES 1 JAR
OR SMALL BOTTLE —

100 g (3½ oz) wild strawberries (top up this amount with regular strawberries, if needed)

1 teaspoon granulated sugar

175 ml (6 fl oz) white wine vinegar

Wild marjoram

Marjoram is a commonly used herb across Europe (where it is more often known as oregano) and it is particularly prevalent in Greek and Italian cooking. *Origanum vulgare* is native to the British Isles. It can be used both fresh and dried – the flavour actually gets stronger as it dries, making it a rare exception in the kitchen.

GROW

Sow wild oregano seeds indoors in late winter – they need warmth to germinate. Thinly sprinkle seeds onto a pre-watered tray filled with a 4:1 mix of multipurpose compost and perlite, then cover with a thin layer of soil. Sit on a bright, warm windowsill out of direct sunlight – better still, use a propagator if you have one.

Transfer seedlings into small pots filled with a 4:1 mix of compost and horticultural grit once the first two true leaves have formed, then pot on into larger pots (preferably terracotta) once the plants are well-established. Position in full sun.

CARE

Water regularly during hot periods, but don't overwater. Feed with a slow-release fertiliser in late spring, then cut back plants in winter. Sit the pot in a sheltered spot; established plants will send up new growth in spring.

EAT

Fresh leaves and flowers are great scattered on pizzas or bruschetta, or stirred into pasta dishes. Pair with summery seasonal ingredients such as tomatoes, courgettes (zucchini) and aubergines (eggplants). Tie up bundles of leaves (still on stems, with flowers) with string and hang in a sunny spot or greenhouse to dry. Bundles will be ready to use by early autumn (fall) and they can be scrunched over pumpkin before roasting, or used to flavour comforting pasta dishes, breads or tarts.

WILDLIFE

Origanum vulgare will bring many familiar pollinators into the garden, including honeybees, butterflies and hoverflies. Many of these species need all the help that they can get. As it's a native plant, having it in the garden can only be a good thing.

CAUTIONS

Marjoram is a common culinary herb and there are few concerns regarding its use in the kitchen.

Wild mushroom and marjoram tart

I tend to make this recipe as one tart but it's just as easy to make individual ones – simply quarter the pastry after unrolling and follow the recipe in exactly the same way.

SERVES 4 —

375 g (13 oz) ready-rolled puff pastry sheet

1 tablespoon rapeseed (canola) oil

300 g (10½ oz) mushrooms (I like to use ceps, but chestnut mushrooms are equally tasty)

3 tablespoons crème fraîche

50 g (2 oz) Parmesan, finely grated

2 teaspoons Dijon mustard

1 large garlic clove, finely grated

small bunch wild marjoram leaves, finely chopped, plus extra to serve

flaky sea salt and freshly ground black pepper

1 egg, beaten

STEP 1 —

Roll the pastry out onto a large baking sheet and gently score a light border 1 cm (½ in) from the edge with a knife (take care not to cut all the way through). Use a fork to prick the pastry inside the border, then chill the base in the refrigerator for 30 minutes.

STEP 2 —

Warm the oil in a frying pan, then fry the mushrooms for 5–7 minutes on a medium heat until they've taken on a little colour and there is no liquid left in the pan. Set to one side.

STEP 3 —

Preheat the oven to 180°C (350°F/gas 6). Mix the crème fraîche, Parmesan, mustard, garlic and wild marjoram together in a bowl, then season to taste. Spread the mixture onto the base, then top with the mushrooms. Brush the tart edge with the egg, then bake for 20–25 minutes until risen and golden. Finish with a scattering of wild marjoram leaves.

Perennial wall rocket

Diplotaxis tenuifolia is the naturalised wild cousin of salad rocket (*Eruca sativa*). It is native to the Mediterranean and Western Asia and has a far more peppery punch than its cultivated relative. I first gathered it in the wild on a rocky slope in Malta – the heat nearly blew my head off, but pick young leaves and the spiciness is far gentler.

GROW

While wall rocket is a perennial plant, I prefer to grow it as an annual with a cut-and-come-again approach to gathering leaves – aim to get two to three harvests out of one sowing. Plant seeds in late spring for outdoor crops in summer and again in early autumn (fall) for an indoor supply throughout winter and early spring.

Thinly sow seeds in pots filled with a 4:1 mix of compost and horticultural gravel, then cover with a thin layer of soil. The seeds need heat as well as light to germinate; it's worth starting them indoors in spring if it's still a bit chilly outside. Thin seedlings to 5 cm (2 in) apart (don't waste them; they're perfectly edible) and position in full sun.

CARE

Keep rocket well-watered during hot periods – it does love warm weather, though, and will thrive during a heatwave.

EAT

Wall rocket can be used in much the same way as salad rocket, but a little goes a long way – in this respect it is far better incorporated into a leafy salad ensemble with other greens than eaten on its own. Use it in pestos, salsas and gremolatas, mix it into savoury tart fillings, stir-fries or scatter a handful of freshly picked leaves on pizzas before serving. Flowers are also edible.

WILDLIFE

Wall rocket flowers will attract a number of pollinating insects to the garden, in addition to several butterflies and moths.

CAUTIONS

Seek professional advice before eating perennial wall rocket if taking prescribed medication.

Perennial wall rocket and charred lettuce picada

Picada is an essential part of Catalan cuisine. Not entirely dissimilar to pesto, it has a variety of uses in the kitchen. Spoon it over grilled fish and meat, or stir it into spicy stews and soups at the last minute.

MAKES 1 JAR —

1 small baby gem lettuce, quartered lengthways

125 ml (4 fl oz) extra virgin olive oil, plus extra to brush the lettuce

1 medium slice white sourdough bread, toasted

80 g (3 oz) perennial wall rocket leaves

50 g (2 oz) blanched almonds, toasted

1 garlic clove, roughly chopped

sea salt and freshly ground black pepper

STEP 1 —

Brush the lettuce quarters with oil then use a hot griddle pan or barbecue to briefly char on all sides. Take care not to cremate the lettuce; a bit of smoky colour and caramelisation is what you're after. Transfer to a plate and leave to cool.

STEP 2 —

Tear the toasted bread into pieces, then add to a food processor, along with the rocket, lettuce, almonds, garlic, oil and a good pinch of salt and pepper. Whizz everything together – not too much, though, as you're looking to retain a bit of texture. Spoon into a sterilised jar. The picada will keep in the refrigerator for a couple of weeks.

Greater reedmace

Many foragers worry about gathering reedmace in the wild. Before it flowers, the stems of *Typha latifolia* look a lot like those of yellow flag iris (*Iris pseudacorus*) and the two often grow cheek by jowl along riverbanks and pond edges. While yellow flag iris isn't deadly, blistered lips and a burning sensation in the mouth and throat is not the kind of thing your guests will want to experience when invited over for a foraged supper. While I feel confident identifying reedmace when out foraging, I have also grown it in baskets in my pond for a number of years – it is very easy to grow, and it tastes great.

GROW

Plant reedmace in late winter. Young plants are readily available online and in specialist aquatic stores. A 10-litre (2.6-gallon) pond basket will house up to three plants – the plant will grow to over a metre in height and it needs a sturdy base to prevent it falling over in the wind. Pot up using aquatic compost, then cover the soil with a layer of washed agricultural grit. Sit the pot in a pond or water-filled container, no deeper than 60 cm (24 in) beneath the surface of the water. Reedmace prefers full sun.

CARE

Reedmace requires little in the way of ongoing care. If growing in a container pond, try to use rainwater and avoid topping up with tap water if possible. If this is the only option, use a dechlorinating liquid – this is as much about encouraging and sustaining native wildlife in the aquatic environment as it is about maintaining the health of the plant. Oxygenating companion plants such as spiked water milfoil (*Myriophyllum spicatum*) and hornwort (*Ceratophyllum demersum*) will help to keep the water healthy, while any dead leaves or sticks that blow into the water should be removed. Trim back any dead, withered growth in late winter – the plant sends up new shoots in spring.

EAT

Reedmace pollen can be gathered in early summer from the top of the flower spike – use as a flour substitute or sauce thickener. The best part of the plant is the starchy root, which is best harvested from autumn (fall) through to early spring, before the flower begins to grow.

The inner stem, or 'heart', is nutritious. Carefully remove plants from the pond basket and wash well with cold water before removing the outer layers – a bit like you would when preparing a leek. The hearts have a fresh crunch and are great in stir-fries, braised or blended into soups.

WILDLIFE

Any healthy pond will become a magnet for wildlife. Reedmace stems and leaves provide perfect cover for dragonflies and damselflies, offering a sheltered spot for larvae to emerge from the water out of the sight of predatory birds.

CAUTIONS

Reedmace roots have a reputation for piercing pond liners; if you are worried about this, sit the pond basket inside a larger container before lowering into the water, or place it on a slate or tile. Seek medical advice before using if taking regular prescribed medication.

Reedmace, grapefruit and fennel salad

A simple early spring recipe, using fresh, vibrant ingredients.

SERVES 4 AS A SIDE —

400 g (14 oz) reedmace hearts

1 grapefruit, peeled and sectioned

1 small fennel bulb, thinly sliced

½ red onion, thinly sliced

2 handfuls of rocket leaves

FOR THE DRESSING —

3 tablespoons olive oil

2 tablespoons cider vinegar

sea salt and freshly ground black pepper

STEP 1 —

Cut the reedmace hearts into 1-cm (½-in)-thick rounds, then steam or boil until tender. Set aside to cool, then add to a salad bowl, along with the grapefruit, fennel, onion and rocket.

STEP 2 —

Mix the oil and vinegar together in a small bowl, then season with salt and pepper. Gently toss the salad in the dressing, then serve.

Watercress

I find watercress all the time when I'm out foraging. It spills out of cool, shallow streams and shady pond edges for most of the year. I'd love to be able to collect a bowlful, give it a quick rinse and eat it there and then. Sadly, I've been gathering wild food for long enough to know that this is rarely an option. Liver fluke is a tiny, but serious parasite that infects livestock such as sheep and cattle; patches of water can host it via run-off from fields and humans can also become infected by eating uncooked wild watercress. Thankfully, watercress is incredibly easy to grow at home, is safe to eat and is at its best immediately after picking.

GROW

Sow watercress in early spring. Fill a pot or container (not too deep) with multipurpose compost, then give it a good soaking with water. Scatter seeds thinly over the wet soil, then cover with either a thin layer of vermiculite or compost. Sit the pot in a shallow tray or container of water, to keep the soil wet. Position in partial shade.

CARE

Change the water once or twice a week to keep it fresh and bacteria free. When harvesting, cut stems back with scissors to about 8 cm (3⅛ in) above soil level, just above a leaf node. Plants should grow back to provide a second harvest; sow new seeds into the pot every few weeks to ensure a continual supply of watercress throughout the season.

EAT

Freshly picked watercress has a peppery kick and there are few salads that don't benefit from its inclusion. It has affinity with red meat (steak in particular), but also pairs well with fish such as salmon or trout. Yield depends on the number of seeds sown and size of container that the plant is grown in, but in the event of a bumper harvest, the leaves can be also used in soups.

WILDLIFE

Watercress is visited by a variety of pollinating insects including bees and hoverflies. The leaves become bitter when the plant is in flower, so I tend to leave it alone for garden wildlife if I've missed it coming into bloom.

CAUTIONS

Seek medical advice before eating if taking prescribed medicine or suffering from kidney problems.

Crushed roasted new potatoes with a watercress dressing

These potatoes are the perfect accompaniment to a spring meal – I like to serve them with roast trout or salmon, plus plenty of seasonal veg.

SERVES 4 AS A SIDE —

FOR THE ROASTED POTATOES —

30 g (1 oz) unsalted butter

2 tablespoons rapeseed (canola) oil

zest of 1 lemon, pared with a potato peeler

12 unpeeled garlic cloves, crushed

750 g (1 lb 10 oz) unpeeled new potatoes

sea salt and freshly ground black pepper

FOR THE WATERCRESS DRESSING —

small bunch of watercress, finely chopped (including stalks)

6 tablespoons rapeseed (canola) oil

2 tablespoons white wine vinegar

STEP 1 —

Preheat the fan oven to 180°C (350°F/gas 6). Add the butter, oil, lemon zest and garlic to a large baking tray, then warm in the oven until the butter has melted. Add the new potatoes to the tray, then give everything a good mix together. Roast the potatoes on the middle shelf of the oven for 30 minutes, then gently crush the potatoes in the tray with a potato masher. Roast for a further 20 minutes, or until golden and crispy. Scatter over a good pinch of salt and pepper.

STEP 2 —

To make the dressing, mix the watercress, oil and vinegar together, then season with salt and pepper. Spoon the dressing over the potatoes and serve immediately.

Sweet violet

The violet was French Emperor Napoleon Bonaparte's favourite flower. During his first exile, supporters in France were able to secretly pledge allegiance to him by wearing violets in buttonholes, or fastened to hats. It's not hard to see why he was so enamoured with them. Delicate and beautiful, sweet violets are one of the first wild plants to flower in the year, making them an early stop in the floral calendar. The flowers have a fragrance and flavour that is unique, while the leaves are also edible.

GROW

Sow sweet violet seeds in autumn (fall). Thinly sow into pre-watered trays filled with a 4:1 mix of compost and perlite; cover with a thin layer of soil then sit the tray outside in a sheltered but bright part of the garden. Keep the soil moist during winter; seed germination can take up to 2 months.

Transfer seedlings to large pots or containers after the first two true leaves have formed, spacing plants approximately 15 cm (6 in) apart. Use a 4:1 mix of humus-rich compost and horticultural sand. Position in partial shade or shade – not too dark, though, as they need plenty of light to be able to thrive.

CARE

Viola odorata is typically a plant of early spring and will have offered up its rewards before many other plants have even stirred into life. Cut back established violets to roughly 5 cm (2 in) above soil level after flowering; this will encourage new growth and hopefully a second harvest of leaves for summer salads. Water well during hot spells and try to avoid exposure to prolonged periods of direct sunlight – violets are cool-weather plants and I speak from experience in saying that too long in the blazing July sun can render them lifeless and half dead. A feed with liquid fertiliser in spring will help to stimulate leaf and flower growth, while mulching with leaf mould in autumn (fall) will give the roots a good nutrient boost.

Violets are stoloniferous plants that will spread around the pot using little runners that root themselves in the soil, or by self-seeding. Well-established containers of sweet violets can get a bit overcrowded, but this can be rectified by dividing plants in autumn (fall).

EAT

Young leaves are a welcome addition to salads early in the year when leafy greens (both wild and from the veg patch) are notably thin on the ground. Flowers are highly fragrant and can be infused into syrups and vinegars, whizzed into sugars, crystalised or simply scattered onto dishes straight after picking – both savoury and sweet.

WILDLIFE

Violets bloom very early in the year, which makes them a valuable source of nectar for any overwintering woodland butterflies that may have stumbled out of hibernation a little hastily, such as the speckled wood (*Pararge aegeria*).

CAUTIONS

Eat leaves in moderation and seek medical advice before using if pregnant, breastfeeding or taking prescribed medication.

Gin and lime granita with a sweet violet syrup

Some think of violet as an acquired taste, and while it is uniquely floral, the sharp citrus pop of lime in this recipe balances it perfectly.

STEP 1 —

First, make the violet syrup. Remove the calyxes (the green bit that holds the flower together) from the violets and place the petals into a heatproof bowl. Pour over the boiling water, cover with a clean tea towel (dish towel) and leave to infuse for 24 hours. Strain the purple liquid through a fine sieve into a small saucepan, then stir in the sugar. Stir on a low heat until the sugar has dissolved – take care not to let the liquid get too hot otherwise you'll lose the beautiful violet colour. Remove from the heat and set aside to cool. If not using immediately, decant into a sterilised bottle and keep in the refrigerator.

STEP 2 —

To make the granita, heat the water in a pan, add the sugar and stir on a medium heat until dissolved. Remove from the heat, stir in the gin, lime zest and juice and allow to cool. Strain the liquid through a sieve, pour into a container and freeze overnight. To serve, scratch at the frozen surface with a fork and scoop into little chilled glasses. Finish with a drizzle of violet syrup.

SERVES 4 —

FOR THE SYRUP —

15–20 sweet violet flowers

75 ml (2½ fl oz) boiling water

150 g (5 oz) caster (superfine) sugar

FOR THE GRANITA —

200 ml (7 fl oz) water

100 g (3½ oz) caster (superfine) sugar

100 ml (3½ fl oz) gin

zest and juice of 4 limes

Wood sorrel

I've always thought that wood sorrel was a beautiful plant, but since I've been growing it at home I've become all the more aware of its unusual, delicate character. *Oxalis acetosella* forms clumps of bright green trefoil leaves in early spring, then sends up tiny white flowers until early June. At night, the heart-shaped leaf lobes fold downwards like tiny umbrellas, while the flowers also close. Come the morning, the leaves lift towards the light and the flowers open. At times it almost feels cruel to eat them, but you never need many leaves and once established they'll continue to send up new shoots.

GROW

In autumn (fall), plant rhizomes 3 cm (1 in) deep in a 4:1 mix of humus-rich compost and horticultural sand. Tuck the pot or container away into a sheltered, shady corner. I find that my little pot of wood sorrel does best when left to its own devices; often I'll forget about it during the winter, only remembering that it is there when leaves start poking up in spring.

Alternatively, wood sorrel can be grown from seed. Germination is most successful from fresh seed harvested from existing or wild plants at the end of summer and sown straight away. Thinly scatter seeds in trays filled with a 4:1 mix of compost and perlite, then lightly cover with soil. Sit the tray on a bright windowsill out of direct sunlight and keep the soil moist. Young seedlings should be overwintered indoors, then transferred into pots in spring once the last frosts have passed. Position plants in shade.

CARE

Wood sorrel doesn't like waterlogged soil, but equal care should be taken to avoid it drying out during hot, dry periods. A small feed with liquid fertiliser in spring will give it a boost, while a layer of leaf mould in autumn (fall) will provide additional nutrients to the rhizomes. Well-establish clumps of wood sorrel can be divided and repotted in winter.

EAT

Carefully pick sorrel leaves, include the stalk but ensure that the rhizome isn't tugged up – a pair of small scissors works best. The leaves have a sharp, lemony pop that makes the mouth water – they make an excellent garnish for both savoury and sweet dishes.

WILDLIFE

Wood sorrel doesn't seem to have a great number of wild visitors, but I have seen honeybees visiting early flowers. Flowers later in the season are cleistogamous; they tend to be hidden, don't open fully and self-fertilise.

CAUTIONS

All sorrels contain oxalic acid, which gives the leaves their sour, tangy flavour, and should always be eaten in moderation and avoided if suffering from arthritis, gout or kidney stones.

Ember-cooked scallops with wood sorrel butter

I love cooking over an open fire. Try to use hand-dived scallops for this recipe if possible; it is a far more sustainable way of fishing for them.

SERVES 4 AS A STARTER —

60 g (2 oz) unsalted butter, at room temperature

1 garlic clove, finely chopped

small bunch of wood sorrel leaves, finely chopped, plus extra to serve

sea salt and freshly ground black pepper

4 large scallops, with shells

TO SERVE —

squeeze of lemon juice

STEP 1 —

Spoon the butter into a pestle and mortar, then add the garlic, wood sorrel, a pinch of salt and pepper. Pound for a few minutes until well mixed.

STEP 2 —

Place each scallop in a shell, then spoon over the herby butter. Carefully sit the shells on the embers of a fire or barbecue, then cook for 4–6 minutes. Cooking time can be shorter or longer depending on the heat of the fire; the scallops should be lightly charred, no longer translucent and the butter should be bubbling. Serve with a squeeze of lemon juice and a generous scattering of wood sorrel leaves.

Common lime

Common lime is one of those trees that you'll probably pass a dozen times each morning on your way to work without realising that it's there. It's a mainstay of city parks and leafy streets. Also known as linden, *Tilia x europaea* is a hybrid of small-leaved lime (*Tilia cordata*) and large-leaved lime (*Tilia platyphyllos*). It grows comfortably in a large pot and is a welcome addition to any garden and, in turn, kitchen.

GROW

Lime trees send up countless suckers and finding one of these is your best bet with regards to growing your own. Look for suckers in spring; they are essentially baby trees growing up from horizontal roots at the base of an established tree. Select a healthy stem and loosen the soil around the base with a clean trowel. Gently lift the sucker and any roots, then use a sharp pair of secateurs to sever it from the parent tree (cover the main root with soil afterwards). Plant the sucker into a pot filled with a 4:1 mix of multipurpose compost and horticultural grit, then water in well. Sit in a warm, bright spot out of direct sunlight. Transfer to a larger pot once the tree is established and a good root system has formed.

CARE

Trees will need staking for the duration. Watch out for aphids; they can quickly spread across a tree and secrete a sticky honeydew – which, while only cosmetic, is not really the kind of thing that you want to have to wash off before eating. Water trees regularly during hot periods; a light prune in winter may be helpful to retain shape.

EAT

Young leaves have a cool flavour with notes of melon and cucumber. I find that they work particularly well with delicately flavoured seafood such as trout or crab. Leaves also respond well to brining – a bit like vine leaves. The flowers, while fleeting, can be used in hot drinks.

WILDLIFE

Lime flowers have a powerful scent that drifts on the breeze and they attract a wide variety of pollinating insects. There is a lot of discourse surrounding whether the nectar is toxic to bees, but based on personal experience, they seem to be – how can I put it – just a bit stoned. Lime flowers contain farnesol, an organic compound that can have a sedative effect. I once experimented with a lime flower, red valerian (*Centranthus ruber*) and honey infusion before bedtime; it totally knocked me out until morning. I was a new father at the time, and my wife quickly alerted me to the fact that I hadn't been much help with the baby during the night!

CAUTIONS

While there are few known side effects linked to the consumption of lime leaves, there is no denying that the flowers can cause drowsiness, so exercise caution if planning to drive or operate machinery after using.

Smoked duck with common lime, melon and pickled blackberries

I'm convinced that lime leaves taste a bit like melon, so why not plate them up with the real thing? Smoked duck brings an earthy note to proceedings, while the acidity of the pickled blackberries cuts through the sweetness.

SERVES 4 AS A STARTER —

FOR THE PICKLED
BLACKBERRIES —

> 100 ml (3½ fl oz)
> red wine vinegar
>
> 100 ml (3½ fl oz)
> water
>
> 40 g (1½ oz) caster
> (superfine) sugar
>
> 200 g (7 oz)
> blackberries

FOR THE SALAD —

> ½ gala melon,
> deseeded
>
> 200 g (7 oz) smoked
> duck, thinly sliced
> (use prosciutto if
> you can't find this)
>
> bowlful of young
> common lime leaves
>
> 2 tablespoons
> pickled blackberries
>
> 2 tablespoons
> olive oil
>
> 1 tablespoon white
> wine vinegar
>
> sea salt and freshly
> ground black pepper
>
> pinch of sumac

STEP 1 —

Tip the vinegar, water and sugar into a saucepan and bring to a near-simmer. Put the blackberries in a heatproof bowl, then pour over the hot pickling liquid. Leave to cool overnight, then transfer the berries and liquid into a sterilised jar. Store in a cool, dark place until ready to use.

STEP 2 —

Use a melon baller to scoop little rounds of melon, then plate up, along with the duck, lime leaves and pickled blackberries. Mix the oil, vinegar and a pinch of salt and pepper together in a small bowl, then spoon the dressing over each plate. Finish with a sprinkle of sumac.

Fennel

Fennel is native to the Mediterranean but has become naturalised in many parts of the world. I wouldn't be without it in the garden; not only is it a go-to culinary herb, but it's also beautiful to look at – tall, architectural stems and bright yellow flowers in late summer that entertain a diverse hub of nectar-loving insects.

GROW

Sow seeds indoors in late winter – they can be harvested easily from wild plants or purchased online. Young fennel roots don't like being disturbed, so choose a large pot or container that will house the plants for the duration. Sow thinly onto a well-drained, pre-watered 4:1 mix of multipurpose compost and agricultural grit; lightly cover the seeds with a thin layer of soil, then position by a bright window or on a ledge in a greenhouse. Germination normally occurs between 7 to 14 days after sowing.

Thin seedlings to about 10 cm (4 in) apart, then gradually harden off outside after the last frosts have passed. Alternatively, grow a single plant in the pot, which in turn will grow much larger than multiples.

CARE

Fennel will tolerate a reasonable amount of drought, although when grown in a pot the long tap root is unable to reach down into the earth in search of moisture, so it is advisable to keep it watered during dry spells. Feed at fortnightly intervals during summer to boost growth. Carefully snip off seed heads to prevent the plant self-seeding around the garden; when the foliage begins to die back in winter cut back hard – it'll grow back again the following spring. Dry the stems and keep hold of them; they're great thrown on embers to add a smoky fennel note to fire-cooked fish. Seed heads should not be composted.

EAT

Lacy fennel leaves, or fronds as they are more commonly known, can be picked from early spring through to dieback in winter. They have a gentle aniseed tang that pairs perfectly with fish, whether it is stuffed in the cavity before cooking or served as part of an accompanying side dish. Fronds can also be finely chopped for use in sauces, dressings and infusions. Tender young leaf stalks can be chopped and sautéed, or left whole and used as a vegetable in their own right.

Flowers can be used to finish dishes, or added to rubs and marinades. Wild fennel seeds are an essential part of the spice cupboard and can be added to curries, chutneys, breads, charcuterie and many other meat, fish and vegetable dishes.

WILDLIFE

Fennel flowers attract a host of pollinating insects – particularly hoverflies. Hoverflies are widely overlooked in the garden and are often feared by people, which is unfortunate, but ultimately what they want. Many mimic the warning colouration of bees and wasps; this is known as Batesian mimicry, named after the British naturalist H. W. Bates, who is considered to be the first person to observe unrelated species having evolved to mimic harmful ones as a form of anti-predator adaptation.

CAUTIONS

Fennel is part of the *Umbelliferae* family, which includes carrots and celery – avoid if aware of a hypersensitivity to these vegetables.

Pork and wild fennel burgers

These burgers are great cooked on the barbecue; if you pick the fennel seeds not long after flowering they are stronger in flavour, with an almost grassy back note.

SERVES 4 —

1 tablespoon rapeseed (canola) oil

1 white onion, finely chopped

1 teaspoon wild fennel seeds

500 g (1 lb 2 oz) good-quality pork mince (aim for a 20–25 per cent fat content)

pinch of chilli flakes

small bunch wild fennel fronds, chopped

splash of dry white wine

sea salt and freshly ground black pepper

TO SERVE —

4 floury white burger buns

4 teaspoons onion marmalade

2 tablespoons garlic mayonnaise

1 small apple, cored and thinly sliced

small bunch watercress leaves

STEP 1 —

Heat the oil in a pan, then cook the onions for 15–20 minutes on a low heat until softened, sticky and golden. Take your time; it's easy to want to rush this step, but the sweet caramelisation achieved by slowly cooking the onions really boosts the flavour of the burgers. Remove from the heat and leave to cool.

STEP 2 —

Toast the fennel seeds in a dry, heavy-bottomed pan until fragrant, then add to a large mixing bowl, along with the pork, cooled onions, chilli flakes, fennel fronds and wine. Season with salt and pepper, then use your hands to mix everything together. Shape into four patties, then griddle or barbecue the burgers for 5–7 minutes on each side, until cooked through. If making in advance, refrigerate the burgers until ready to use, but let them sit at room temperature for 15 minutes before cooking.

STEP 3 —

Lightly toast the burger buns, then coat the lids with the onion marmalade. Spread the mayonnaise on the bottom halves of the buns, then add the burgers, apple slices and watercress. Top with the bun lids.

Dandelion

Dandelions are one of the first wild flowers to bloom and their cheerful early presence is a sure sign that spring is on the way. It is likely that their name is derived from the French *'dent de lion'*, which simply translates as *'tooth of lion'* – a reference to the jagged edges of the leaves. At a time when salad crops are few and far between, *Taraxacum officinale* is a late-winter mainstay when the rest of the garden has yet to stir into life.

GROW

Dandelions are incredibly easy to grow and will crop all year round if sown indoors (do wait until the frosts have passed if growing outside). Sow seeds onto pre-watered compost, then lightly cover with soil – they require light to germinate. Germination should occur 7 to 21 days after sowing.

Thin seedlings to 10 cm (4 in) apart if growing for buds, flowers and roots; don't thin if growing for young leafy greens.

Dandelion leaves can be bitter, which is not to everyone's taste. Reduce bitterness by covering with a large cloche or pot (cover any holes), to block out all light. Leave for a couple of weeks but keep the pot watered; this will blanch the leaves, turning them pale and reducing astringency.

CARE

Water regularly and deadhead flowers to avoid the plant self-seeding. Dandelions are perennials; if a healthy root network has been established during the year, they are likely to survive the winter, although they are so easy to grow that it's not too much of a tragedy to start again the following spring, if needed.

EAT

All of the plant is edible – roots, leaves, flower buds and flowers. Roots can be used in teas, thinly sliced and added to salads or chopped and used in stir-fries. Roots can also be roasted and ground into a coffee substitute, while flower buds can be pickled and used in place of capers.

Flowers and young leaves make for a welcome addition to salads. Flowers can also be used in teas or infused into syrups. Leaves can be steamed and sautéed and are especially good with bacon.

WILDLIFE

Dandelions are one of the first plants to flower in early spring, when many bees are beginning to emerge from hibernation. The flowers are also a good source of food for beetles, butterflies and hoverflies.

CAUTIONS

Dandelion is a member of the *Asteraceae* family, which includes ragwort (*Senecio jacobaea*) and daisies (*Bellis perennis*), which have been known to cause allergic reactions in some people. As always when trying a new food, eat a tiny amount first, then wait 24 hours before consuming again. Seek advice before eating if pregnant or breastfeeding.

All parts of the plant are known to have diuretic properties, so think twice about tucking a few leaves into a sandwich before setting off on a long car journey!

Dandelion, taleggio, bacon and grape pizzetas

These little pizzetas work on a number of levels; they are tangy, salty and sweet, balanced by the bitterness of the dandelion leaves.

STEP 1 —

Mix the yeast and 50 ml (1¾ fl oz) of the water together in a small bowl, then leave in a warm spot for 10–15 minutes until bubbly. Mix the flour and salt together in a large mixing bowl, then add the bubbling starter, remaining water and oil. Use your hands to bring everything together into a ball, then knead on a floured surface until the dough is smooth and elastic. Brush a clean bowl with oil, pop the dough inside, cover with cling film (plastic wrap) and leave until doubled in size.

STEP 2 —

Fry the lardons in a pan until crispy, then set to one side.

STEP 3 —

Preheat the fan oven to 200°C (400°F/gas 7). Place a pizza stone on the top shelf of the oven; if you don't have one, a lightly floured baking tray will do. Knock the dough back, then divide into six equal-sized balls. Roll the balls out on a lightly floured work surface into 15-cm (6-in) rounds, then top with the taleggio, bacon and grapes. Bake the pizzetas for 10–15 minutes, or until golden and the cheese is bubbling. Finish with a good grind of black pepper and a scattering of dandelion leaves.

MAKES 6 —

1 teaspoon fast-action yeast

250 ml (8½ fl oz) warm water

400 g (14 oz) strong bread flour

1 teaspoon fine salt

1 tablespoon olive oil, plus extra for oiling

150 g (5 oz) smoked bacon lardons

200 g (7 oz) taleggio, sliced

150 g (5 oz) red seedless grapes, halved

freshly ground black pepper

large handful of young dandelion leaves, washed

Dog rose

I grow a number of cultivated roses at home, but for all their breadth of colour, habit and scent, I still think that our native wild rose is one of the best. Flowers appear in early summer – simple, pale pink blooms that attract bees and insects in droves, intoxicated by their sweet scent. Come autumn (fall) the shrub is set with ruby-red seed pods, or hips as they are more commonly known. These hips will often remain on the branches throughout winter, providing much-needed colour when everything else seems a bit grey and pallid.

GROW

Take semi-ripe cuttings from a parent plant from late summer through to very early autumn (fall). Use secateurs to cut 25–30-cm (10–12-in) lengths from vigorous, healthy-looking stems that have grown during the current season. Make a horizontal cut below a bud for the base of the cutting, then cut above a bud at a 45-degree angle for the top. Remove all but a few leaves at the top of the cutting.

Dip the cuttings in hormone rooting powder, then gently push into pots filled with a 1:1 mix of multipurpose compost and horticultural grit, leaving one-third of the stem length exposed above the surface of the soil. Space cuttings 15 cm (6 in) apart if planting multiples. Water in well, then transfer to a bright and airy spot – warm, but out of direct sunlight. Most of the cuttings should have taken root by late autumn (fall) but will need overwintering somewhere relatively mild and frost-free. Ensure that they don't dry out during the winter months.

The following spring, pot on young plants into large pots filled with a 4:1 mix of compost and horticultural grit. Position in full sun.

CARE

Dog rose is a vigorous, thorny climber that requires a sturdy structure to scramble up and hold shape when grown in a pot. A tall wigwam of coppiced hazel sticks or bamboo canes will be more than adequate; tie in new growth with string and trim off any unruly stems that get carried away at the top.

As with many roses, *Rosa canina* will benefit from regular feeds with a liquid rose fertiliser while it is putting on new growth in spring. Keep well-watered during hot periods. Prune in winter; use sharp secateurs to remove any dead stems and cut stems back to about 50 cm (20 in) above soil level to retain shape and encourage vigorous growth the following spring. Cut just above an outward facing bud eye at a 45-degree angle.

EAT

Flowers make for a pleasing addition to salads; they can also be candied to decorate cakes and desserts by brushing in egg white and dusting with caster (superfine) sugar. Rosehips can be made into syrups, cordials, fruit leathers and jellies; they are packed with vitamin C and a daily spoonful of rosehip syrup during the winter months can give the immune system a much-needed boost.

WILDLIFE

The size of a dog rose will be led by age and pot size, which will in turn dictate flower and fruit yields. Resisting the urge to harvest every single rosehip from the shrub in the autumn (fall) is a good thing; birds such as thrushes, waxwings and goldfinches will be glad of the food when the ground is frozen and insects are scarce. Many pollinating insects will take advantage of the attractive flowers in summer, while the thorny tangle of branches will offer small mammals and birds protection from predators.

CAUTIONS

Rosehips can help to a maintain a healthy immune system, but seek medical advice before consuming if suffering from kidney stones. Wear gloves when preparing the hips as the tiny seed hairs can irritate skin (many people will remember them as a natural itching powder from their school days). Seek professional advice before eating if using specific medication, or pregnant or breastfeeding.

Apple and rosehip jelly

I'll often spread this jelly on toast in the morning, but it's also great in glazes and sauces. Try it on crackers with a sharp, hard cheese, such as Manchego.

STEP 1 —

Roughly chop the apples – no need to peel or core them. Give the rosehips a quick blitz in a food processor, then add both to a saucepan. Cover with water (bring the water level up to about 2 cm (¾ in) above the fruit), then bring to the boil. Simmer for 45 minutes, or until everything is soft and pulpy. Remove from heat, stir in the sweet cicely leaves (if using), then leave to infuse for 20 minutes. Pour the fruit and liquid into a jelly bag, then leave to drip through – preferably overnight.

STEP 2 —

Measure out the liquid, then add the sugar – approximately 80 g (3 oz) for every 100 ml (3½ fl oz) of liquid. Stir in the honey and lemon juice (include any seeds; they contain pectin, which will help the jelly set), then bring to the boil. Boil the liquid hard until it reaches 220°C (430°F) when tested with a jam thermometer. If you don't have a thermometer, spoon a dollop onto a chilled plate and leave it for a minute or two. Push it with your finger – if it wrinkles, the jelly will set when cooled. Pour into a sterilised jars, seal and store in a cool, dark shelf or cupboard.

MAKES 1 JAR —

500 g (1 lb 2 oz) apples (any type will do)

250 g (9 oz) rosehips

handful of sweet cicely leaves (optional)

granulated sugar

1 tablespoon honey

juice of ½ lemon

Sea beet

Sea beet has good culinary heritage, being the genetic ancestor of all cultivated types of beetroot (beet), Swiss chard and sugar beet. It is a common coastal plant across Europe through to North Africa and Asia but will also grow in gardens – salinity is not a prerequisite. *Beta vulgaris maritima* is the first thing I look for when I get out of the car at the beach; many would argue that it should be the buckets and spades or ice-cream van, but there you go. The nearest beach is over an hour's drive from my house, so it seems perfectly reasonable to want to grow it at home.

GROW

Sea beet is common in many coastal areas and it is legal to collect seed in late summer (as with all foraging, use discretion and only take a small amount). Alternatively, seeds can be sourced online, as can young plants. Sow seeds in spring, using trays filled with a 4:1 mix of potting compost and perlite. Sow seeds approximately 3 cm (1⅛ in) apart, then cover with a thin layer of soil. Water well, then leave in a greenhouse or bright and airy windowsill, out of direct sunlight.

Transfer seedlings into small pots, using a 3:1 mix of multipurpose compost and horticultural sand. Pot on plants into large, deep containers once they are established with a good, healthy root system.

CARE

Water sea beet regularly during hot spells. The plant will benefit aesthetically from a little tidy once in a while – the outer leaves often start to look a bit tired and take moments to trim off. Weekly feeds with liquid seaweed in late spring will set the plant up for the summer. Move to a sheltered spot during the winter months; sea beet is hardy and should withstand a relatively cold winter.

As a relative of Swiss chard and beetroot (beet), sea beet can be prone to some of the pests and diseases that can affect traditional veg patches. Keep an eye out for tiny white eggs on the undersides of leaves; these are the eggs of the beet-leaf miner (*Pegomya hyoscyami*), the larvae of which can burrow into leaves, leaving unsightly brown leaf blisters. The eggs are easily scraped off gently with the back of a fingernail.

EAT

The great thing about sea beet is that larger leaves taste just as good as smaller ones – if not better. Strip off the woody middle stems before cooking. Use sea beet leaves as you would spinach or chard, in quiches, stir-fries and pasta dishes.

WILDLIFE

Sea beet can host a number of rare beetles, plus the larvae of the nationally scarce rosy wave moth (*Scopula emutaria*).

CAUTIONS

As with all members of the beetroot (beet) family, sea beet should be consumed in moderation. Seek medical advice before eating if receiving treatment for kidney stones.

Sea beet stuffed mussels

There's a bit of prep involved in this recipe but it's well worth it; serve these mussels with a chilled glass of white wine, such as Chablis.

STEP 1 —

De-beard the mussels and discard any with broken shells. Heat 1 tablespoon of the oil in a large pan with a lid, then stir in the shallot. Cook for a minute, then add the mussels and wine. Pop the lid on, then steam on a medium heat for 2–3 minutes, until the mussels have opened. Discard any that haven't opened. Strain the mussels in a large colander, reserving 50 ml (1¾ fl oz) of the cooking liquor. Set the mussels aside to cool.

STEP 2 —

Pour the cooking liquor into a frying pan, then add the sea beet. Cook on a medium heat for 5–7 minutes, or until the leaves have wilted. Leave to cool, then squeeze out as much liquid as you can from the sea beet.

STEP 3 —

Add the bread, sea beet, garlic, remaining oil and a pinch of salt and pepper to a food processor, then whizz briefly until you have a breadcrumb-like consistency. Remove the meatless half of the shell from each mussel, then sit the remaining halves on a baking tray (pan). Top each mussel with a spoonful of the stuffing, then drizzle over the melted butter. Cook under a hot grill for 5 minutes, then serve immediately.

SERVES 2 AS A STARTER —

1 kg (2 lb 4 oz) large live mussels

5 tablespoons rapeseed (canola) oil

1 shallot, finely chopped

small glass of white wine

50 g (2 oz) young sea beet leaves

50 g (2 oz) stale sourdough bread

2 garlic cloves, chopped

sea salt and freshly ground black pepper

50 g (2 oz) unsalted butter, melted

Juniper

Think of growing *Juniperus communis* as more of
a long-term project, one that will hopefully help
a species that is in decline. Juniper is one of only
three conifer species native to the UK and numbers
have dropped hugely over the last 30 years. Habitat
loss, overgrazing and disease are major contributing
factors, but the fact juniper is dioecious (requiring
both male and female trees to produce berries)
hasn't helped its cause. It is a pretty, evergreen
shrub, and while it may be a little wait for berries,
a pair of potted trees will complement any patio
or garden.

GROW

Seed germination can be a lengthy affair, so it is preferable to grow juniper from semi-ripe cuttings or obtain small plants from specialist nurseries. To grow edible cones (or berries, as we know them) a tree of each sex is required; female plants only produce fruit after being wind-pollinated by a male. Use sharp, clean secateurs to take cuttings in late summer or early autumn (fall), approximately 15 cm (6 in) in length. Make sure to cut from the main middle shoot on a branch, as juniper remembers its growth direction and a side shoot will grow out of the pot at an angle. Remove roughly one-third of the needle-like leaves at the base of the stem, dip the cuttings in hormone rooting powder then insert into pre-watered pots filled with a 4:1 mix of compost and perlite. Cover with a propagator lid or polythene, then sit in a bright warm spot such as a windowsill or greenhouse, out of direct sunlight. Water regularly and move them outside in spring.

Pot on established juniper plants into large pots or containers filled with a 3:1:1 mix of multipurpose compost, ericaceous compost and horticultural grit. Ensure that there are plenty of holes in the bottom for good drainage. Position in full sun.

Juniper berries ripen over 2 to 3 years, which may sound a bit alarming, but they ripen at staggered intervals; there will be a point where the plant will be producing flowers, new berries and ripe berries simultaneously, so regular harvests will be possible after an initial wait.

CARE

Juniper can withstand a relative amount of drought, but do water it regularly during hot periods. Little pruning is required, other than a little tidy here and there to retain shape.

EAT

Juniper berries can be used to flavour stocks, marinades and sauces, or can be ground to use as a pepper-like seasoning. They are great in casseroles and have a particular affinity with game – rabbit and venison in particular. Berries can also be used in desserts, and as one of the primary botanical flavours in gin, it comes as little surprise that they lend themselves to drinks and cocktails. Needles and stems removed when pruning can be saved for use in small-scale hot smoking.

CAUTIONS

As a precaution, the consumption of juniper berries should be avoided during pregnancy.

Juniper-crusted pork chops with mustardy cannellini beans

Cannellini beans are probably my desert-island legume; I cook with them pretty much all year round and they are spot on for this dish, which uses juniper berries to flavour the meat. This a great weeknight supper for two, possibly best saved for when there is a nip of autumn in the air.

SERVES 2 —

FOR THE CHOPS —

- 2 teaspoons whole juniper berries
- 2 teaspoons sea salt
- 1 teaspoon freshly ground black pepper
- 2 pork chops
- 2 tablespoons rapeseed (canola) oil

FOR THE BEANS —

- splash of white wine
- 1 garlic clove, sliced
- 1 small white onion, chopped
- 400 g (14 oz) tin cannellini beans, drained and rinsed
- 200 g (7 oz) spinach leaves (use nettles, borage or sea beet if growing)
- 100 ml (3½ fl oz) chicken stock
- 1 teaspoon Dijon mustard
- 2 tablespoons crème fraîche

STEP 1 —

Toast the juniper berries in a heavy-bottomed pan until fragrant, then crush them with a pestle and mortar, along with the salt and pepper. Brush the chops with tablespoon of the oil, then sprinkle over the juniper seasoning, ensuring that the meat is well coated.

STEP 2 —

Heat the remaining oil in a non-stick pan to a medium-high temperature, then cook the chops for approximately 7 minutes on each side, or until cooked through. Transfer the meat to a plate, then cover loosely with kitchen foil and a tea towel (dish towel).

STEP 3 —

Reduce the hob to a medium heat, then deglaze the pan with the white wine. Stir in the garlic and onion and cook for 8–10 minutes until softened. Add the beans, spinach and stock, then bring to a simmer. Remove the pan from the heat, then stir in the mustard and crème fraîche. Give everything a good stir, season to taste, then serve with the pork chops.

Hops

While hops are native to the British Isles, many of the bines that are to be found winding their way through hedgerows in the wild are escapees from the once-thriving hop industry, which peaked in the 19th century, but dwindled towards the latter part of the 20th. Hop shoots are the most expensive vegetable in the world in terms of weight; in countries like Belgium where they are more regularly eaten you can expect to pay a hefty €1,000 (£865) for a kilo. It makes perfect sense to grow and harvest your own at home. *Humulus lupulus* is a relatively low-maintenance plant and the busy network of leaves that it produces each year are great for wildlife.

GROW

Hops can be grown from seed, but I prefer to start them from rhizomes, which are readily available online and are far easier to grow. Plant individual rhizomes in spring after the frosts have passed, 7.5 cm (3 in) deep in a large pot or container (the bigger the better), using a 3:1:1 mix of multipurpose compost, ericaceous compost and horticultural grit. Sit the pot against a sunny wall or fence (south facing is preferable), then water in well. *Humulus lupulus* bines need somewhere to scramble up; the best options are either a wooden trellis or lengths of thick garden twine attached horizontally to a wall or fence. If the container is freestanding, a wigwam of tall sticks will suffice.

CARE

Leave the plant to its own devices in its first year to allow a decent root network to form. My potted hop is 2 years old; last year it grew happily but conservatively – this year it returned with startling vigour and has completely covered the fence at the bottom of the garden. Make sure that the soil doesn't dry out during hot periods; regular feeds in spring with an all-purpose liquid fertiliser will stimulate growth. Cut back all growth to soil level in late autumn (fall) when the leaves start to brown.

EAT

Young leaves can be added to salads and they are perfectly edible, albeit in a slightly uninspiring kind of way. It's the shoots that we're here for. Hops send up slender, asparagus-like tendrils from early spring through to midsummer. Many foraging guides wax lyrical about hop shoots being an exclusively spring treat, but as I sit here writing in late June my hop is still producing tender new shoots and they are just as tasty as the ones I harvested a couple of months ago. Use scissors to cut roughly 15-cm (6-in) tips from the plant and try to eat them as soon as possible. They are truly delicious; soften for a minute in a little butter, or stir into pasta dishes and risottos. Hop shoots also ferment well, while flowers later in the season on female plants can be infused into hot drinks or used in small-scale beer production.

WILDLIFE

A well-established hop creates a dense microclimate that is highly valuable to insects. Butterflies, moths, bees, hoverflies and beetles will all take advantage of the enclosed habitat that it provides; I have just been out to inspect my plant and a tiny lesser garden spider (*Metellina segmentata*) is spinning a delicate web among the leaves and stems in the sunshine.

CAUTIONS

Seek guidance from your doctor if eating regularly alongside prescribed medication or are pregnant/breastfeeding.

Homemade crumpets with shrimps and hop shoots

I used to think that life was too short to make your own crumpets – then I made my own crumpets and I have to say that I'm a complete convert. Hop shoots are one of my favourite wild ingredients and this recipe really does them justice.

STEP 1 —

Tip the flour into a large mixing bowl. Dissolve the sugar in the warm milk, then add the yeast. Set aside for 10 minutes, then mix into the flour with a wooden spoon. Beat the mixture for 3–4 minutes until you have a smooth batter. Cover the bowl with cling film (plastic wrap) and leave in a warm place for about an hour.

STEP 2 —

Stir the baking powder and salt into the warm water. Mix it into the batter. Cover loosely with a tea towel (dish towel) and leave in a warm place for a further 15 minutes.

STEP 3 —

Set a flat griddle or heavy-based frying pan on a low heat, then brush with melted butter. Grease the insides of two non-stick crumpet rings, then sit them on the pan. Spoon 2 tablespoons of the batter into each ring, then cook for 8–10 minutes until the crumpets have risen, the tops look set and bubbles have popped on the surface. Flip the crumpets over carefully with a spatula, cook for a further minute, then remove from the heat. Repeat the process with the remaining mixture then allow the crumpets to cool completely.

STEP 4 —

Toast the crumpets under a hot grill while you prepare the topping. Heat the butter, shrimp, garlic and mace in a pan for a few minutes on a medium heat until the butter starts to bubble, then stir in the hop shoots. Cook for a further 2–3 minutes until the shoots have softened, then remove from the heat. Add the lemon juice, season, then spoon over the crumpets.

SERVES 4
(2 CRUMPETS EACH) —

FOR THE CRUMPETS —

225 g (8 oz) strong white bread flour

½ teaspoon caster (superfine) sugar

300 ml (10 fl oz) warm whole milk

2 teaspoons fast-action yeast

1 tablespoon baking powder

1 teaspoon fine salt

50 ml (1¾ fl oz) warm water

TO SERVE —

generous knob of butter, plus extra for brushing

100 g (3½ oz) brown shrimps

1 small garlic clove, finely grated

pinch of mace

handful of freshly picked hop shoots

juice of ½ lemon

sea salt and freshly ground black pepper

Marsh samphire

I can tell you that it is 37 miles to what I believe to be my nearest patch of wild marsh samphire, and while I'm all for a bit of dedication when it comes to foraging, a two-hour plus round trip makes it a less than regular addition to the menu. I know, I know, samphire is readily available in supermarkets, but seeing it sitting there, dark green, chilled and limp on the fish counter just doesn't do it for me. *Salicornia europaea* should be a vibrant, almost citrus green, with a sweet saline crunch that you only get when eating just-picked. All it takes is a little TLC and you can grow and eat it anywhere – even if you live in Coton in the Elms, Derbyshire, which is the furthest inland point in England and a tarmac-crunching 70 miles from the nearest coastal foraging opportunity.

GROW

Sow samphire seeds in April (they can be purchased online). About a week before planting, fill a seed tray with multipurpose compost. Stir 1 heaped teaspoon of unrefined sea salt and 1 teaspoon of organic liquid seaweed into 1 litre (34 fl oz) of water, then water the tray. Repeat daily; this advance prep helps to establish a good salty environment for seed growth prior to sowing and increases the chances of germination.

Sow the seeds evenly across the tray, then cover with a thin layer of compost. Leave in a warm sunny spot or greenhouse (maintaining a temperature of above 25°C/77°F), watering daily with the salt/seaweed solution. Germination can take up to 20 days or even longer, so be patient. Transfer individual seedlings to larger pots once they are 2–3-cm (¾–1⅛-in) high. Position in full sun.

CARE

I give my samphire plants a good daily soaking in spring and summer; I reason that I'm replicating the tide in doing so, and they seem more than happy. Don't overdo it when harvesting, but cut regularly to keep plants succulent and lush. Snip just above one of the jointed nodes, leaving 1–2 cm (½–¾ in) of fleshy green stem to give plants a good chance of growing back. Plants don't need quite as much watering/feeding with the prepared solution during the winter months – about once a fortnight should keep them happy. Make sure to overwinter pots out of the worst of the frosts.

EAT

Considering that it grows by the sea, it comes as little surprise that samphire works well with seafood. Simple is often the best way – briefly soften in a little butter and serve with fish such as bass and Dover sole, or steam with shellfish such as mussels and clams. Samphire can be stirred into fillings for quiches and tarts, and it also works well when pickled. Take care not to over-season when using *Salicornia europaea* in the kitchen – in pretty much all cases you don't need as much salt as usual.

WILDLIFE

In its native environment, the seeds of marsh samphire are often eaten by wading birds. There is no denying that when grown in pots the plant is in a relatively alien environment, so in this respect it is unlikely to encourage much in the way of native wildlife.

CAUTIONS

Often when gathering marsh samphire in the wild one must consider the cleanliness of the estuary that it has grown in, but this is not an issue when growing the plant at home. Seek medical advice before eating if using prescribed medicine. Samphire is available in many supermarkets and fishmongers and there are few concerns regarding its consumption.

Quick-pickled samphire and summer veg

I've listed a few vegetables that I often grow in the garden in this recipe, but this is pretty much a raid-the-veg-patch kind of affair. A handful of halved cherry tomatoes, thinly sliced baby courgettes or cucumbers would also work well in the mix.

SERVES 4 AS A SIDE —

150 ml (5 fl oz) rice wine vinegar

50 g (2 oz) sugar

1 teaspoon flaky sea salt

75 g (2½ oz) marsh samphire

100 g (3½ oz) radishes, thinly sliced

1 medium-sized carrot, cut into ribbons with a potato peeler

1 small red onion, thinly sliced

½ red chilli, deseeded and finely chopped

juice 1 lime

STEP 1 —

Heat the vinegar, sugar and salt in a saucepan until everything has dissolved, then set aside to cool.

STEP 2 —

Blanch the samphire for 1 minute in boiling water, then transfer to a bowl of iced water for 5 minutes before draining in a colander.

STEP 3 —

Mix the samphire, radishes, carrot, onion and chilli together in a bowl, then pour over the pickling liquid and lime juice. Leave everything to infuse and mingle for at least 30 minutes before serving.

Sweet cicely

One of the more troublesome aspects of foraging in the wild is that it can be a rather unforgiving hobby when one gets it wrong. This is a genuine concern when hunting for and identifying wild mushrooms, but there are also issues regarding the *Umbelliferae* family, of which sweet cicely is a member. Sweet cicely is a perennial herbaceous plant that is common in many woodland areas and dappled grassy verges, but as with its fellow edible cousin cow parsley (*Anthriscus sylvestris*), it bears a striking similarity to hemlock (*Conium maculatum*) – the consumption of which could well dispatch you into the realm of 'rookie ex-forager' with an alarming degree of haste.

When you buy a packet of seeds and watch a plant grow, there can be little doubt as to what will be served up on the plate. Young sweet cicely plants can also be purchased from specialist nurseries – either way, this is a delicious and versatile addition to the herb garden.

GROW

Sow sweet cicely in autumn (fall) – seeds need cold stratification in order to germinate. The plant doesn't like being uprooted after germination, so sow straight into small pots, using a 4:1 mix of multipurpose compost and perlite. Tuck the pots away in a sheltered but bright spot for the winter. Make sure that the soil doesn't dry out.

Pot on established plants into large deep pots that will accommodate a tap root, filled with humus-rich compost. Position in partial shade or shade, but never in full sun.

Sweet cicely can also be grown from seeds harvested freshly from the plant in autumn (fall); they germinate better than dried seeds and there is no need for stratification. A 100 per cent positive identification of the parent plant is a must.

CARE

Cicely likes moist soil, so keep it well-watered during the summer months. Remove flower stems if growing primarily for foliage – this will encourage bushier growth.

The plant is likely to die back in winter, although it could well hang on depending on position and weather conditions. Cut back any dead or withered growth, then mulch with a layer of leaf mould. Sweet cicely is hardy, but it pays to err on the side of caution, so move the pot to a sheltered part of the garden until it warms up in spring.

EAT

Cicely leaves have a sweet aniseed flavour and can be used raw to scatter over salads or desserts, or garnish drinks. The leaves and stems contain anethole, an organic compound that acts as a natural sweetener – use them in syrups, compotes and stewed fruit dishes as a low-calorie alternative to sugar. The sharpness of rhubarb and gooseberries is particularly well offset by cicely; the amount of sugar required is notably less and often it isn't needed at all. Flowers can also be used as a garnish, while the green seed pods are more intensely flavoured than the leaves – they too can be chopped and used as a sweetener.

WILDLIFE

Sweet cicely is one of the first plants to flower in spring, which makes it an important source of early nectar for pollinating insects.

CAUTIONS

There are no known side effects from regular sweet cicely consumption. Seek guidance from your doctor if eating regularly alongside prescribed medication or are pregnant/breastfeeding.

Honey-roast rhubarb and sweet cicely fool

This is a great early summer dessert – you could also try it with gooseberries, although you might need an extra spoonful of honey, depending on the sharpness of the fruit.

STEP 1 —

Preheat the fan oven to 160°C (320°F/gas 4). Cut the rhubarb into 4-cm (1½-in) chunks, then transfer to a large, ovenproof dish. Drizzle over the honey, scatter over the chopped sweet cicely, then give everything a quick stir together. Cover the dish loosely with baking parchment then roast for 10–15 minutes, or until the rhubarb is just tender. Leave to cool.

STEP 2 —

Whisk the cream, yoghurt and vanilla essence together until thick and forming peaks. Carefully fold the rhubarb and any juices from the roasting dish into the cream, trying not to break the fruit down too much in the process and reserving a few pieces to top each portion at the end. Spoon the fool into glasses or bowls, then finish with the leftover rhubarb and freshly picked cicely leaves.

SERVES 6 —

500 g (1 lb 2 oz) rhubarb

3 tablespoons honey

5–7 sweet cicely leaves, roughly chopped, plus extra to serve

300 ml (10 fl oz) double (heavy) cream

500 g (1 lb 2 oz) Greek yoghurt

½ teaspoon vanilla essence

Bramble

The next time that you strike gold and hit a patch of the sweetest, juiciest wild blackberries, try to make a note of the spot. Within the subgenus of *Rubus fruticosus agg.*, there are many microspecies, all of which vary in size, texture and taste. This accounts for why some berries found in hedgerows are like bullets, while others taste like the best fruit you have ever eaten. It is essential to take cuttings from the right plant when planning to grow your own.

GROW

Take blackberry cuttings in late winter or early spring – look for healthy-looking, red-green stems with plenty of buds or young leaves. Use sharp secateurs to trim 15–20-cm (6–8-in) lengths from the parent plant. Cut just below a bud at the base of the cutting and just above a bud at the top. Use a sharp knife to gently scrape the epidermis at the bottom of the cutting – this will help to stimulate root growth. Remove all but a couple of leaves at the top, dip the cuttings in hormone rooting powder then push into pots filled with pre-watered perlite, making a hole with a pencil first. Sit the pots on a bright windowsill or shelf in a greenhouse, water regularly and mist daily with water. New growth should be visible after about 3 weeks – if not sooner.

Carefully remove the rooted cuttings from the perlite and transfer to small pots filled with a 4:1 mix of compost and perlite. Grow on until the young bramble plants are well-established and roots are visible at the bottom of the pot. Transfer individual plants into large pots or containers filled with a 4:1 mix of compost and horticultural grit; brambles have a relatively shallow root system, so go for width over depth when choosing pots. Position in full sun.

CARE

Brambles are essentially biennial plants above ground, growing on a perennial rootstock beneath it. Flowers and fruit form on 2-year-old canes, so don't expect a harvest the first year after planting. Plants need a framework or trellis to scramble over, whether it be a wigwam of sticks or a wooden lattice attached to a wall. Tie in new growth regularly, water well during hot periods and treat plants to a feed with liquid fertiliser in mid-spring.

Cut back second-year growth to soil level after fruiting and mulch pots with well-rotted compost or manure in late winter.

EAT

Flower buds and flowers can be scattered over salads or desserts but remember that picking these will affect fruit yields later in the year. Young leaves can be eaten raw or infused into teas.

Blackberries have an almost infinite amount of uses in the kitchen, whether they be sweet or savoury. Things naturally head towards the more autumnal side of things; a handful of blackberries added to an apple pie will lift it to another level, while the dark sweetness of the fruit lends itself perfectly to game – venison, pigeon and pheasant being but a few of its culinary bedfellows. Blackberry syrups can be used to sweeten stock-based sauces; they can also be measured into a Champagne flute and topped up with fizz.

WILDLIFE

A bramble in bloom on a sunny summer's day will be alive with the hum of bees, hoverflies, butterflies and lacewings. A number of moths, including the beautiful peach blossom moth (*Thyatira batis*), use it as their larval food plant, while small birds may nest in the prickly branches or use them to take refuge from predators. Dormice, foxes and badgers will eat fallen fruit, as will birds (they'll of course take them from the branches too if you're not quick).

CAUTIONS

There aren't any specific concerns linked to the consumption of blackberries, but take caution if allergic to raspberries, cherries or any other fruits in the *Rosaceae* family.

Blackberry and wild chimichurri focaccia

This is very much a savoury recipe despite its fruity addition; the blackberries add little pops of sweetness to the focaccia that work perfectly with the chimichurri.

STEP 1 —

Tip the flour into a large mixing bowl. Add the yeast; mix it into the flour, then add the salt and mix again (adding these separately prevents the salt from killing the yeast). Make a well in the middle of the flour, then pour in the water and 25 ml (1½ tablespoons) of the oil. Mix everything together to make a dough; hands are fine, but the dough is quite sticky – using a plastic scraper is better.

STEP 2 —

Turn the dough out onto a work surface lightly dusted with flour, then pull and stretch it for about 10 minutes until smooth and elastic. Pop the dough into a clean bowl brushed with oil, cover with cling film (plastic wrap) then leave in a warm place for 1 hour, or until the dough has doubled in size.

STEP 3 —

To make the chimichurri, mix the marjoram, rocket, ramsons bulbs, shallots, chilli, remaining oil and vinegar together in a bowl, then season with salt and pepper. Set to one side.

STEP 4 —

Preheat the fan oven to 200°C (400°F/gas 7). Stretch the dough out into a large, 25 x 35 cm (10 x 13¾ in) greased baking tray, cover loosely with a tea towel and leave in a warm place for another 45 minutes, until risen to about half as high again. Gently push the blackberries into the dough, then spoon over three-quarters of the chimichurri. Bake for 25–30 minutes until golden, leave to cool for 20 minutes, then spoon over the remaining chimichurri. Finish with flaky sea salt and edible wild flowers.

SERVES 8–10 —

500 g (1 lb 2 oz) strong bread flour

7 g (¼ oz) fast-action dried yeast

10 g (½ oz) fine sea salt

350 ml (12 fl oz) tepid water

100 ml (3½ fl oz) rapeseed (canola) oil, plus extra for greasing

small bunch of marjoram (use wild marjoram, if growing)

small bunch of rocket (use perennial wall rocket, if growing)

2 ramsons (ramps) bulbs

2 shallots, finely chopped

1 green chilli, deseeded and finely chopped

30 ml (1 fl oz) white wine vinegar

sea salt and freshly ground black pepper

200 g (7 oz) blackberries

TO SERVE —

flaky sea salt

borage, wild marjoram and wild fennel flowers (optional)

Sea kale

I've had good success with growing potted sea kale as a perennial vegetable. Much like marsh samphire and many other coastal greens, *Crambe maritima* is a halophyte; it will grow happily in saline environments, which is why it can often be found growing on the beach when little else is to be found nearby. There are good reasons to grow your own. Sea kale is part of a globally rare and threatened habitat called 'vegetated shingle', for which the UK is a stronghold. and must not be picked without the permission of the landowner. Over-harvesting and transferring plants to gardens during the Victorian era is cited as the main reason for its scarcity, while all-too-common habitat loss is also a contributing factor.

GROW

Sow sea kale seeds in March. If growing seeds harvested from the wild, you'll need to remove the corky outer shell that is effectively a buoyancy aid – apply pressure with a rolling pin or back of a trowel to crack the casing and remove the seed, a bit like how you'd extract the kernel from a nut. Seeds are only viable for about a year, so if you've gathered a small pocketful while out on a beach walk you may as well sow them all. Seeds can also be purchased online.

Soak the seeds in water for 24 hours before sowing; this helps to increase the chances of germination. Plant seeds 2 cm (¾ in) deep in small pots filled with a 4:1 mix of compost and perlite, water well and sit on a bright windowsill or shelf in a greenhouse. Don't let the soil dry out.

Pot on established plants into large, deep pots that will accommodate a tap root, using a 4:1 mix of compost and horticultural sand. It is unlikely that sea kale grown in a container will reach the size that it can achieve in the wild but given sufficient root space it will be more than content in a pot.

CARE

Water well during hot spells and treat plants to a fortnightly feed with liquid seaweed throughout the summer months. Plants may die back in winter; mulch with a layer of leaf mould and tuck the pot away in a sheltered spot out of the worst of the weather until spring, when it should send up new shoots.

EAT

Leaves can be harvested and eaten up until the plant comes into flower; young shoots are the best but try to pick with restraint to prevent damaging the plant in the long term. Leaves can be steamed, blanched or sautéed and are best served simply – often a little melted butter and a pinch of sea salt is more than enough. Young flower buds are delicious and can be used in a similar way to purple sprouting broccoli. Flowers have a honey-like fragrance and work well in salads or scattered over cooked fish.

WILDLIFE

Sea kale entertains many of the same guests that visit cabbages in the veg patch and whether one welcomes them or not is a point of discretion. Beetles, weevils, slugs and caterpillars may all frequent; if they are to be removed from the plant, ensure that they are transferred to a suitable alternative food plant.

CAUTIONS

The mineral content of sea kale leaves may have diuretic properties.

Sea kale with a date and yoghurt dressing

I use this dressing on all kinds of dishes, but there's no denying that it works best on plates that feature earthy, iron-rich vegetables such as Swiss chard, beetroot (beet) or kale.

SERVES 2 AS A SIDE —

FOR THE DRESSING —

> 3 plump medjool dates, stoned
>
> 1 small garlic clove
>
> salt and freshly ground black pepper
>
> 4 teaspoons natural yoghurt
>
> 1 tablespoon rapeseed (canola) oil
>
> zest and juice of ½ lemon

FOR THE KALE —

> 10–12 young sea kale stems
>
> 50 g (2 oz) unsalted butter

STEP 1 —

First, make the dressing. Finely chop the dates, garlic and a pinch of salt on a board, mixing everything together as you do so and using the flat side of the knife to work everything into a paste. Transfer to a bowl, along with the yoghurt, oil and lemon zest and juice. Thin the dressing with a little water if necessary, to achieve a drizzling consistency. Season to taste with salt and pepper.

STEP 2 —

Blanch the sea kale in boiling water for 1 minute, then pat dry with kitchen paper. Melt the butter in a frying pan, then sizzle until it takes on a nutty brown colour. Add the stems and cook for 2–3 minutes. Remove from the heat and serve hot, with a drizzle of the dressing.

Alexanders

Alexanders is a naturalised relic of Roman occupation. A popular herb and vegetable for hundreds of years, it was usurped in the kitchen by celery and subsequently made its way to the coast (who can blame it), where it is to be found in great profusion. It also grows inland but is less frequent; having said that, only last week I was walking along a street in south-west London when I happened upon a fine patch of *Smyrnium olusatrum*, quite happy amidst the bustle of the city.

GROW

There is need for caution as alexanders are in the same family as hemlock water dropwort, and they could easily be confused. If unsure of their identification, it's worth buying rather than foraging the seeds to grow. Although when in seed, the black, ribbed, crescent-shaped seedpods of alexanders are distinctive.

Alexanders is a biennial. Sow seeds in autumn (fall); they require stratification, and a period of cold is essential for germination in late winter/early spring. Sow in trays filled with a 4:1 mix of compost and perlite; gently press the seeds down to ensure contact with the surface, but don't cover with soil as they require light to germinate. Tuck the trays away in a sheltered but bright corner of the garden and keep the soil moist.

Carefully prick out individual seedlings and transfer to small pots after the first two true leaves have formed. Pot on into large, deep pots filled with a 4:1 mix of compost and horticultural grit once a healthy root system is established. Position in full sun or partial shade.

CARE

Alexanders doesn't require feeding, but keep plants well-watered during hot periods as they don't like to dry out. Remove all seed heads before composting; kept in a sealed jar they are a valuable addition to the spice cupboard.

EAT

As a precursor in the kitchen to celery, it comes as no surprise that alexanders can be used in similar ways. Leaves and stems are notable for their celery-like flavour, but the taste is altogether more complex, with a touch of asparagus and a faintly floral back note.

Pick young side stems in mid-spring – leave the main stem as it can be a bit on the tough side. Alexanders stems can be steamed, sautéed or gently braised in savoury dishes. On the sweeter side of the spectrum, they can be candied. Young leaves can be added to salads or chopped and stirred into dishes.

Young flower heads are best cooked just before they open, steamed or sautéed then finished with a little melted butter. They can also be pickled or dipped in a light batter before deep-frying. The roots can also be eaten.

The seeds are possibly my favourite part of the plant. Alexanders was once known as 'black potherb' presumably after the jet-black colour of its dried seeds. Ground in pestle and mortar, they are aromatic, with notes of citrus, cardamom and myrrh. I often use them to spice curries and stews.

WILDLIFE

Alexanders flowers are rich in nectar and their early appearance in spring makes them an important source of food for emerging pollinators such as bees, wasps and hoverflies. Take care not to allow Alexanders to spread into the wild, it can be dominant and shade out smaller, native plants.

CAUTIONS

All parts of alexanders are considered safe to eat but seek medical advice first if planning to use as a medicinal herb and take extra care to test your tolerance if you're allergic to celery, which is in the same family (*Apiaceae*).

Alexanders Seed and Orange Beignets

These little beignets are a bit like doughnuts; the spicy notes of alexander seeds work perfectly with orange.

STEP 1 —

Toast the alexanders seeds in a heavy-bottomed pan until fragrant, then crush with a pestle and mortar. Bring the crushed seeds and coconut milk to a near-simmer in a small pan; remove the pan from the heat, pop a lid on then set aside for the liquid temperature to reduce to warm but not hot.

STEP 2 —

Transfer the infused coconut milk to a mixing bowl, then add the yeast. Set aside for 10 minutes, then add the flour, egg, orange zest and sugar. Mix together to form a dough.

STEP 3 —

Knead the dough on a lightly floured surface for 10 minutes, then place in an oiled bowl. Cover with a clean tea towel (dish towel) and leave in a warm place for 1 hour 30 minutes, or until the dough has doubled in size.

STEP 4 —

Heat the oil to 175°C (347°F). Roll the dough out on a lightly floured surface to a rectangle roughly 25 x 20 cm (10 x 8 in), then cut into 24 smaller rectangles. Fry the beignets in batches, giving them 3–4 minutes cooking time and flipping occasionally with a pair of tongs. Transfer briefly to a plate lined with kitchen paper, then serve warm with a dusting of caster sugar.

MAKES 24 —

2 teaspoons alexanders seeds

200 ml (7 fl oz) coconut milk

1 teaspoon fast-action dried yeast

350 g (12 oz) strong white bread flour

1 egg, beaten

zest of 1 small orange

100 g (3½ oz) caster (superfine) sugar, plus extra for dusting

1 litre (34 fl oz) vegetable oil, for deep-frying

Norway spruce

January is bleak at the best of times (my birthday is towards the end of the month and is often voted the most depressing day of the year), but the general air of back-to-work melancholy is compounded by the sight of countless Christmas trees discarded in front gardens. Much better to grow your own in a pot and bring it in each year, plus you'll be rewarded with lush green edible spruce tips each spring. All members of the spruce family are edible, but the flavour can vary – *Picea abies* is my favourite.

GROW

Small Norway spruce trees can be purchased from nurseries and garden centres all year round, although there is no doubting that greater numbers are available in the run-up to Christmas. Ensure that the tree is pot-grown; often spruce trees are grown in the ground, dug up and transferred to pots to sell during the festive period – these trees have far fewer roots, are weaker and struggle to survive.

Spruce trees can also be grown from semi-ripe cuttings in late summer. Use sharp secateurs to take 15–20-cm (6–8-in) cuttings from an established tree – make sure that they are green at the top and woody at the base. Strip off the needles from the bottom third of the cutting. Fill small pots with a 2:1 mix of compost and horticultural grit, then use a pencil or dibber to make holes in the soil. Insert the cuttings into the holes, water the pots well and sit in a warm, bright spot out of direct sunlight. Keep the soil moist. This method works with all types of conifer and they should be ready to pot on the following autumn (fall).

Pot up young trees in a 3:1:1 mix of humus-rich compost, ericaceous compost and horticultural grit. Cover the holes in the pot with bits of broken terracotta pots or a thin layer of shingle before adding the soil. Water in well and position in full sun.

CARE

Re-pot spruce trees once a year as they get bigger, increasing the pot size gradually each time. Trees will grow happily in pots for several years until they reach a height of about 1.8 metres (6 feet), after which they will need to be planted in the ground. If this isn't an option, it's often worth visiting your local nursery; they may well be happy to exchange your tree for a smaller one and the process can begin all over again.

Trees can be pruned between late winter and early spring. Cut off any dead or yellowing branches. Check the top of the tree to make sure that there is only one strong vertical leader – remove any competitors with a pair of sharp secateurs. Give trees regular feeds during the spring and summer months and remember to water regularly during hot periods.

A spruce tree needs to acclimatise before coming indoors for Christmas, so stagger its journey inside. Move the tree to a sheltered spot in the garden for a couple of days – an unheated greenhouse or conservatory is a better option if available. Give the tree a good water before bringing it indoors; remember not to sit it too close to a radiator or fire. Water regularly during the festive period and repeat the staggering method when moving it back outside.

EAT

Harvest the lush green new growth from the tips of branches in late spring; try to take no more than 20 per cent of the shoots and gather from multiple places to avoid massively impacting the tree's growth. A little goes a long way; a small handful will be more than enough for a number of dishes – they also freeze well.

Spruce tips can be infused into syrups, whizzed into sugars or simply scattered over sweet and savoury dishes. The flavour is bright with a distinct note of citrus; in this respect they pair well with lemons, limes and oranges.

WILDLIFE

Spruce trees offer a habitat for a variety of insects, including beetles, caterpillars and hoverflies.

CAUTIONS

Seek advice from a medical professional before eating regularly if pregnant or breastfeeding.

Lemon and spruce tip crinkle cookies

These little cookies are a great way of cooking with spruce tips – you could also try making them with finely chopped thyme leaves, or rosemary.

STEP 1 —

Melt the butter in a small saucepan, then set aside until cooled but not set. Whisk the egg, yolk and sugar together in a mixing bowl until pale and fluffy, then whisk in the melted butter, a little at a time. Use a spatula or wooden spoon to mix in the lemon juice and zest.

STEP 2 —

Stir the flour, baking powder and spruce tips together in a separate bowl, then mix in the wet ingredients. Use your hands to bring everything together into a ball of dough, but don't overwork it. Wrap the dough in cling film (plastic wrap) and chill in the refrigerator for a minimum of 2 hours before using.

STEP 3 —

Preheat the fan oven to 160°C (320°F/gas 4). Roll the dough into 3-cm (1⅛-in) balls, then roll in icing sugar until they are well covered. Arrange on baking sheets lined with baking parchment – make sure that there is a reasonable space between them as the dough spreads as it cooks. Bake for 10–12 minutes, then cool before serving.

MAKES 16–18 —

115 g (3½ oz) butter

1 egg, plus 1 yolk

125 g (4 oz) sugar

2 tablespoons lemon juice

zest of 1 lemon

250 g (9 oz) plain (all-purpose) flour

½ teaspoon baking powder

1 teaspoon spruce tips, finely chopped

icing (confectioner's) sugar

Stinging nettle

Nettles are a true cut-and-come-again crop; once established, they will repeatedly send up new shoots after harvesting – it is for this reason that many look upon them as a troublesome garden weed. There is no doubting that left unmanaged they can quickly take over, but grown in pots or containers they are perfectly easy to keep in check. I prefer to look upon nettles as a trusted ingredient in the kitchen. They are packed full of vitamin C and are rich in nutrients and antioxidants.

GROW

Sow nettle seeds in spring after the last frosts have passed. Thinly sprinkle seeds onto a pre-watered, 4:1 mix of compost and horticultural sand, then cover with 1 cm (½ in) of soil. Position in a bright, sunny spot and water regularly. Be patient; while it may seem at odds with the plant's ubiquity, nettle seeds can take over a month to germinate – sometimes even longer. Thin seedlings to approximately 5 cm (2 in) apart.

CARE

Resist cutting leaves for the first few months to allow a decent root network to grow. Other than regularly watering during dry periods, nettles need little in the way of care, but keep an eye out for weeds that may start to grow in the pot. Cut back plants in winter and mulch with a layer of leaf mould to give the roots a nutrient boost.

EAT

Pick leaves from mid-spring onwards; regular harvesting stimulates regrowth and the younger leaves are always the best for cooking and eating. Infuse nettle leaves in hot water to make a refreshing tea. The leaves lose their sting so there is no need to worry about risking a stung lip. Leaves can be steamed and sautéed and used in place of spinach in a variety of recipes, blitzed raw in smoothies or juiced.

WILDLIFE

Urtica dioica is a very important food plant for the larvae of a number of butterflies and moths, including the comma, peacock, red admiral, burnished brass, jersey tiger and rather fabulously named snout moth. The plant also provides food for many other insects, which in turn can attract hungry birds, hedgehogs, frogs and toads to the garden.

CAUTIONS

Wear gloves when picking nettles. The leaves have tiny, needle-like hairs on their undersides that pierce the skin and discharge histamine, acetylcholine and serotonin, which in turn cause pain and inflammation.

Raw stinging nettle salad

This recipe is based on a Turkish dish called *sirgan salatasi*, and while it is incredibly tasty, there's no denying that it requires something of a leap of faith in order to take the first mouthful. If the leaves are prepped correctly, there is absolutely no reason why you should get stung!

SERVES 4 AS A SIDE —

FOR THE SALAD —

large bowlful of young stinging nettle leaves, stalks removed

3 tomatoes, deseeded and chopped

¼ cucumber, deseeded and chopped

small bunch of mint leaves (use water mint, if growing), roughly chopped

2 tablespoons pomegranate seeds

100 g (3½ oz) feta, crumbled into chunks

FOR THE DRESSING —

2 tablespoons rapeseed (canola) oil

juice of 1 lemon

sea salt and freshly ground black pepper

TO SERVE —

pinch of sumac (optional)

STEP 1 —

Rinse the nettle leaves in cold water, then drain in a colander. Lay a clean tea towel (dish towel) out on a work surface, then scatter over the nettle leaves. Place another clean tea towel on top, then use a rolling pin to lightly crush the leaves. Be gentle; it's not about pulverising them into submission, more applying pressure to break down the prickly hairs.

STEP 2 —

Stir the dressing ingredients together, then season to taste. Mix the nettle leaves, tomatoes, cucumber, mint, pomegranate seeds and feta together then pour over the dressing. Toss the salad together, then finish with a sprinkle of sumac (if using).

Strettine (nettle tagliatelle)

Don't feel that tagliatelle is the only
use for this pasta dough; it's just as
good used to make ravioli, lasagne or
orecchiette – little ear-like pasta shapes
that are great fun to make with kids.

STEP 1 —

Blanch the nettle tops in a pan of boiling
water for 1 minute, then quickly transfer to a
bowl of iced water. Drain in a colander, then use
the end of a rolling pin to squeeze out as much
water as possible from the cooked leaves.

STEP 2 —

Blitz the eggs, nettles and a pinch of salt briefly
in a food processor. Tip the flour onto a clean kitchen
surface, then make a well in the centre. Pour the egg
and nettle mixture into the well, then use your fingers
to slowly bring everything together. If the dough feels
dry, work in a little extra egg yolk, then knead for
4–5 minutes until smooth and elastic. Cover with cling
film (plastic wrap) then leave to rest for 30 minutes.

STEP 3 —

Roll the pasta out using a pasta machine, a quarter of
the dough at a time. Set the pasta machine to its widest
setting, then feed the dough through slowly. Repeat
the process, narrowing the rollers each time until they
are adjusted to their thinnest setting and the pasta is a
smooth, long sheet. Fix the tagliatelle attachment to the
machine, then cut into ribbons. Cook immediately in
salted water, or hang the strettine in a warm room for
1–2 hours to dry – I drape the pasta on a long stick
balanced between two chairs, but coat hangers will work
just as well. Store in a sealed container until ready to use.

SERVES 4 —

large bowl of young
stinging nettle tops
(roughly 150 g/5 oz)

3 medium eggs (plus
1 yolk, if needed)

pinch of salt

300 g (10½ oz)
'00' pasta flour

Chickweed

It seems a bit unfair that chickweed has 'weed' in its name. I would argue that an appellative makeover is way overdue; there's no denying that it can be troublesome in the garden, yet I grow mine in a container on a patio, never let it go to seed and it hasn't once left its intended vessel. Chickweed is packed full of nutrients and is one of my favourite wild salad greens.

GROW

Sow chickweed in late winter. Thinly scatter seeds in a large container, pot or window box filled with multipurpose compost, then cover with 1 cm (½ in) of soil. Give it a good water, then position on a bright windowsill or shelf in a greenhouse. Germination should be quick; thin healthy seedlings to roughly 10 cm (4 in) apart and keep well-watered. It's well worth hardening off young plants in a cold frame if moving outside after the last frosts have passed. Chickweed isn't particularly fussy; position in full sun, partial shade or shade.

CARE

Keep plants well-watered during hot periods. Gather leaves and stems in the morning when the air is cool (they wilt easily) and refrigerate if not eating immediately. Cut to about 2.5 cm (1 in) above soil level; this will give the plant a chance to grow again for repeat harvests. Chickweed will also spread around the pot via rooting stem nodes, so it won't be long until you have a plentiful pot of greens to harvest from.

EAT

Chickweed leaves are great in salads and sandwiches. Eat the stems too, a bit like how you would with watercress. The leaves can also be chopped and stirred into risottos and pasta dishes at the last minute, or used as a garnish.

WILDLIFE

Chickweed is a food source for a number of species of carabids, including the iridescent green tiger beetle (*Cicindela campastris*). Birds may also eat the leaves, which comes as little surprise given the plant's name – chickweed was once used as a fodder crop for chickens.

CAUTIONS

Chickweed contains saponin, that can be toxic in high quantities, but large concentrated amounts need to be consumed for the plant to be harmful. Any worries need to be viewed in context – other saponin-containing plants include peas, kidney beans, quinoa and asparagus. Seek guidance from your doctor if eating regularly alongside prescribed medication, or if you are pregnant/breastfeeding.

Pigeon and chickweed tagliata

The local wood pigeons have a keen eye and regularly plunder my pots – often in outrageously brazen fashion while I am actually sitting on the little patio where many of the plants are growing (at times, they really do seem to be without fear). It may seem a touch macabre, but pigeon meat works particularly well with chickweed, which is one of their favourites.

SERVES 4 —

8 pigeon breasts

4 tablespoon rapeseed (canola) oil

2 garlic cloves, crushed

1 tablespoon apple and rosehip jelly (redcurrant jelly will work as an alternative)

2 tablespoons balsamic vinegar

sea salt and freshly ground black pepper

100 g (3½ oz) freshly picked chickweed stems with leaves

250 g (9 oz) cherry tomatoes, halved

50 g (2 oz) Parmesan, shaved

TO SERVE —

crusty bread

STEP 1 —

Season the pigeon breasts with salt and pepper, then set to one side. Heat 1 tablespoon of the oil with the garlic in a frying pan, then fry the pigeon for 3 minutes on each side. Transfer the meat to a plate and leave to rest for 5 minutes.

STEP 2 —

Remove the pan from the heat, then add the jelly, remaining oil, balsamic vinegar and any juices from the pigeon plate. Whisk everything together to make a warm dressing – season with salt and pepper, then remove the garlic.

STEP 3 —

Thinly slice the pigeon breasts, then arrange on plates along with the chickweed and tomatoes. Spoon over the dressing, then finish with the Parmesan shavings. Serve with crusty bread.

Pink clover

Red clover? Pink clover? *Trifolium pratense* is often called by both names – to me the flowers have a gentle magenta hue, so I'm going with pink. Pink clover is easy to grow, and alongside dandelion it is a great plant for young children to nurture when they're starting off on their home-grown wild-flower journey. The flowers are also very near the top of many pollinating insects' list of must-have nectar sources, which makes it an all-round winner in the garden or in the corner of a terrace or balcony.

GROW

Sow pink clover in spring, after the last frosts have passed. Thinly sow into deep trays or containers filled with a 4:1 mix of compost and horticultural grit, then cover with a 1-cm (½-in) layer of soil. Water in well, then position on a bright windowsill or shelf in a greenhouse. Plants will do just as well indoors as they will outside after germination – just ensure that they are positioned in full sun.

CARE

Clover needs regular watering and will not tolerate dry soil. Last summer I foolishly neglected my watering duties for a couple of days during a hot spell (why would I do such a thing?!); to my horror, the pot quickly became a withered shadow of its former self, but I managed to rescue it by moving it quickly into a shady spot and quenching its thirst with a thorough watering. Feed regularly with liquid fertiliser during the spring and summer months. *Trifolium pratense* is a perennial herbaceous plant and will grow back each year if cared for properly – cut foliage back once it starts to brown then tuck the container in a sheltered spot out of the worst of the frosts for the winter.

EAT

Flowers can be used in salads as a garnish, or in hot infusions, cold drinks and syrups. They have an agreeable floral, slightly pea-like flavour, which is unsurprising as clover is a member of the pea family – *Leguminosae*. Leaves can also be used in salads.

WILDLIFE

If there is one flower that honeybees (in fact, all bees) love, it is clover. Farmers and beekeepers often benefit mutually from the positioning of beehives near field of clover. Bees pollinate the flowers, which in turn allows the plant to sow seed and spread. The nectar makes great honey, while the plant fixes nitrogen in the soil, which can reduce the need for synthetic fertilisers. The more bees in the garden the merrier, in my opinion, so start sowing!

CAUTIONS

Always seek medical advice before using, if taking prescribed medicine or are pregnant or breastfeeding.

Pink clover lemonade

This lemonade is so simple to make and is a real thirst quencher. A few strips of thinly sliced root ginger work well in here too if you have them at hand.

STEP 1 —

Heat the clover flowers and water gently in a large saucepan; stir intermittently until the pan reaches a near-simmer, then kill the heat (keep a lid on the saucepan between stirs and after cooking). Stir in the honey, leave to cool, then strain the liquid through muslin (cheesecloth) into a large bowl. Squeeze in the lemon juice, then chill the lemonade in the refrigerator.

STEP 2 —

Give the mint leaves a scrunch in your hands then tear into the bottom of a jug or pitcher. Add the sliced lemon and a good handful of ice cubes, then top up with the chilled lemonade.

MAKES 1 BOTTLE —

medium bowlful of fresh pink-clover blossoms

1 litre (34 fl oz) water

5 tablespoons honey

juice of 2 large lemons

small bunch mint leaves (use water mint, if growing)

1 lemon, thinly sliced

ice cubes

Ramsons (Europe) / Ramps (US)

The culinary profile of ramsons (and ramps, their American cousins) has grown considerably over the last decade and for good reason. Nothing says spring more than the scent of garlic in the air at my go-to spot down by the river; it feels like the kind of ingredient that everyone should be able to enjoy when it is in season and thankfully it is very easy to grow in a pot or container. I use an old bucket with a few holes drilled in the base, but anything will do as long as the soil is kept moist and it is positioned out of direct sunlight.

GROW

Ramsons and ramps can be grown from seed; however, it takes several years for bulbs to establish themselves and return a decent crop. It is a far better idea to establish a colony of plants in a large pot or container in year one by planting bulbs. Seeds from these plants can be collected in early summer, then redistributed among the existing bulbs to increase the density (and in turn yield) of the patch over time. Bulbs for both plants are readily available online or can be gathered from the wild in autumn (fall) with the landowner's permission. Once established, they will also produce new bulbs underground.

Sow bulbs in autumn (fall) approximately 8 cm (3⅛ in) deep in a good humus-rich compost, spacing bulbs 3–4 cm (1⅛–1½ in) apart. Position in a shady corner of the garden; ensure the soil doesn't dry out over the winter months, but also that the bulbs don't sit in soggy soil. Shoots should be visible in early spring. Position in shade.

CARE

Gather with restraint; if all leaves are removed the bulbs will struggle to come back again the following year. Harvest seed pods once they have formed; loosely wrap in muslin then hang in a greenhouse or sunny spot to dry. Extract the seeds and use for cooking, or sow back into the soil (lightly cover with 1 cm (½ in) of compost if doing so).

Water regularly during the spring months when growth is at its peak. After dieback, tuck the pot or container away in its shady spot, but don't let it dry out during hot spells. Mulch with a good layer of leaf mould in late winter.

Well-established pots may need dividing, which should be done in autumn (fall). Carefully pull apart tightly packed clumps of bulbs by hand, then transfer into new pots.

EAT

All parts of the plant are edible. Young leaves are better for eating raw, while older leaves lend themselves to being cooked or blitzed into sauces. Flowers are great to scatter over salads and risottos. Pickle young seed pods and use in place of capers. Bulbs can be harvested in autumn (fall) and used in exactly the same way as garlic cloves, but remember that by doing so yields will be reduced the following spring.

WILDLIFE

Ramsons and ramps flowers are listed as important early blooms for pollinators such as bees, hoverflies and beetles.

CAUTIONS

Seek medical advice before eating if taking prescribed blood-thinning medication.

Fermented ramsons butter

Possibly not one for date night; there's no denying that this butter is very ripe and very garlicky. I have a confession to make: I photographed this garlic baguette alone in the studio and promptly ate the whole thing soon after, with almost delirious abandon.

STEP 1 —

To make the ramsons purée, blanch the ramsons for 30 seconds in a pan of salted boiling water, then quickly transfer to a bowl of iced water using a slotted spoon. Leave for a few minutes, then drain the leaves in a colander. Pat dry with kitchen paper, then blitz in a food processor with the oil. Let the green oil drip through a jelly bag or coffee filter into a bowl, then decant into a sterilised bottle – the oil will keep in the refrigerator for a few weeks. Scoop out the drained purée from the jelly bag/coffee filter and transfer to a bowl.

STEP 2 —

Stir the puréed ramsons, rice flour, salt and sugar together, then use a digital pH meter to test acidity. Add lemon juice gradually in small amounts, mixing it in thoroughly and re-testing each time until the purée has a pH of between 4 and 4.5. This adjustment creates the perfect environment for fermentation but also ensures that the purée is acidic enough to prevent any harmful bacteria forming. Transfer to a sterilised jar or small container with a lid and sprinkle a light layer of sea salt on top of the purée. Pop the lid on and leave to ferment out of direct sunlight for 3–5 days, depending on preference for ripeness. Pop the lid once a day during fermentation to let out any pressure build-up and keep in the refrigerator once it's ready.

STEP 3 —

To make the flavoured butter, melt the butter in a small saucepan, remove from the heat and leave to cool for 5 minutes. Stir in the fermented ramsons purée, transfer to a bowl or container then chill until set and ready to use.

MAKES APPROX.
250 G (9 OZ) —

FOR THE FERMENTED
RAMSONS PURÉE —

150 g (5 oz)
ramsons leaves

250 ml (8½ fl oz)
rapeseed (canola) oil

2 teaspoons
rice flour

1 teaspoon flaky
sea salt, plus
extra for storing

½ teaspoon caster
(superfine) sugar

lemon juice

FOR THE FERMENTED
RAMSONS BUTTER —

250 g (9 oz)
unsalted butter

2 tablespoons
fermented
ramsons purée

Ramsons and Comté gnocchi bake

It's easy to be lulled into thinking that we've seen the end of the cold, wet weather when spring arrives. This baked gnocchi dish is comforting, rich and flavoursome – perfect for when Mother Nature sees fit to put the sunshine and warmth on hold.

STEP 1 —

Preheat the fan oven to 180°C (350°F/gas 6). Cook the gnocchi in salted water, drain and spread out onto a baking tray to prevent the pieces sticking together.

STEP 2 —

Melt the butter in a saucepan, then quickly mix in the flour to form a smooth paste. Keep the pan on a medium heat and gradually add the milk, stirring briskly with a balloon whisk as it thickens. Add 75 g (2½ oz) of the cheese and continue to stir for a few minutes until melted. Remove the pan from the heat and set aside to cool for 5 minutes.

STEP 3 —

Add the ramsons leaves and cheese sauce to a food processor, season with salt and pepper, then blitz until well mixed. Stir the gnocchi and green sauce together, then spoon into an ovenproof pan or dish.

STEP 4 —

Sprinkle over the remaining cheese, then bake in the oven for 30–35 minutes until golden and bubbling. Finish with a scattering of ramsons flowers.

SERVES 6 —

750 g (1 lb 10 oz) potato gnocchi

30 g (1 oz) unsalted butter

30 g (1 oz) plain flour

500 ml (17 fl oz) milk

125 g (4 oz) Comté, grated

large handful of ramsons leaves, roughly chopped

sea salt and freshly ground black pepper

TO SERVE —

ramsons flowers

Ramsons kimchi

This recipe is not for the faint-hearted – the chilli flakes pack a real punch. I often add a little of my ramson kimchi to a cheese toastie, or spoon it into egg fried rice at the last minute. It can really lift a straightforward lunch or supper into something rather noteworthy.

MAKES 1 MEDIUM JAR —

35 g (1 oz) glutinous rice flour

75 g (2½ oz) gochugaru (Korean red chilli powder)

25 g (1 oz) sea salt

35 g (1 oz) caster (superfine) sugar

2 garlic cloves, roughly chopped

thumb-sized piece of ginger, peeled and roughly chopped

1 small apple, cored and roughly chopped

1 small white onion, roughly chopped

large bowlful of freshly picked ramsons leaves, washed

½ sweetheart cabbage, thinly sliced

STEP 1 —

Add the rice flour and 250 ml (8½ fl oz) of water to a small pan, then bring to a bubble over a medium heat; whisk regularly until it thickens to a paste. Leave to cool to room temperature.

STEP 2 —

Blitz the cooled rice paste, gochugaru, salt, sugar, garlic, ginger, apple and onion in a blender. Don't worry if there are a few rogue chunks of apple or onion in the paste – nothing too big, though.

STEP 3 —

In a large bowl, use your hands (I recommend wearing rubber gloves) to massage the paste into the ramsons leaves and cabbage. Take care not to crush the leaves, but ensure that they all get a good coating. Transfer to a large jar, top up with 150 ml (5 fl oz) water (boiled first, then cooled) and leave to ferment out of direct sunlight for 3–5 days, depending on how ripe you like your kimchi. Refrigerate once you're happy to halt further fermentation – it will keep for a few months if properly chilled.

Acknowledgements

I would like to thank above all the following people: my wife Victoria and our children Amélie, Rafferty and Oscar – the best gardening companions and recipe tasters that a person could wish for. Also, Mum, Dad, Jenny, Ian, Carla, Bettina, Damien, Ross and John for their unfaltering support. Thanks to all of the team at Hardie Grant – especially Eve, Eila, Bonnie and Amelia for making the book look so beautiful, and to my foraging chum Sarah Watson for casting an objective eye over the manuscript.

This book is for Carla; her watering can is always half full and she shares my enthusiasm for a good patch of Ramsons.

About the Author

Stuart Ovenden is a professional photographer and author based in Hampshire, with a passion for wildlife, all things foraged and simple, seasonal food.

@stuovenden